THE MYTH OF
Free Will

ALSO BY CRIS EVATT

How To Organize Your Closet...and Your Life!
How to Pack Your Suitcase and Other Travel Tips
Simply Organized!
Opposite Sides of the Bed
30 Days to a Simpler Life
The Givers & The Takers

THE MYTH OF
Free Will

CRIS EVATT

Café Essays

SAUSALITO

Café Essays

SAUSALITO, CA

info@CrisEvatt.com

Cover Illustration by New Vision Technologies, Inc.
Einstein Illustration by Christine Fusco

THIRD EDITION

Library of Congress Control Number: 2007906990
ISBN 978-0-9708181-8-8

For Lovers of Reality

Contents

A Short Quiz

Here are a few issues which we are going to explore in this book. It might be interesting for you to jot down a few notes prior to reading. On a separate sheet of paper, write down one or two sentences in answer to the following questions:

- What is free will?

- If you think you have free will, why do you think so?

- What is causality and determinism?

- What are the benefits of believing in free will?

- What are the costs of the belief?

Fold up the paper with your answers and tuck it into the back of this book. When you finish reading, look at them again, and see if your thinking has been influenced by what you've read.

Foreword

Does everyone wonder about free will? Certainly the world's great thinkers have struggled with the problem, as have the scientists, philosophers and psychologists gathered together in this delightful collection. Indeed, free will is said to be the most discussed philosophical problem ever. But it's not a problem we should leave to philosophers, for it concerns us all, tangling as it does with issues of morality, wisdom and the meaning of life.

In fact, I suspect that at some level everyone who thinks at all must have asked themselves questions such as Who am I? Why do I end up doing things I didn't want to do? Is everything inevitable, and if so why should I bother doing anything at all?

To my surprise, I recently discovered that even my dad asks these questions.

My father is not an educated man. He left school at fifteen, fought in the Second World War, came home to take over his father's printing business and, as far as I know, never read a book the rest of his life. He did not share my mother's strong Christian faith, which provoked endless arguments between her and me, nor did he enjoy discussing life, the universe and everything. Looking back, I see him as a straightforward, honest and kindly man, a father I could admire, but not one I could share my ideas with—not someone I thought would have anything to say about free will. But I was wrong, as I learned one evening, having a drink by the fire with him before I set off to give an evening lecture.

"Where did you say you were going dear?" he asked for the third or fourth time.

"To Sharpham House. It's a Buddhist meditation retreat center near Totnes."

"Why are you going there?"

"I'm giving a lecture on free will."

"Free will? What is there to say about that?"

How do you explain the problem of free will to a man of ninety who has advanced dementia, just about knows who you are, and whose world consists of not much more than a bed, a fireside chair, and the daily paper he can no longer understand?

I did my best. I said that it seemed to me that my body and brain are clever machines that can function perfectly well without there being any inner me, or spirit or soul, to direct them. So there is a problem—I seem to be in control but I cannot really be. This is, I said, what I was going to be talking about.

To my complete surprise this set him alight. He was quite sure that he had, or was, such an inner spirit; it stood to reason, he had to be. I asked him where this spirit came from, and he said from God. I protested that there was no God, and that spirits controlling a body would have to be magic, and he came back with a comment I have never forgotten.

"If there is no spirit, then why do we want to be good?"

He didn't ask why we are good, or argue about good and evil, he simply asked, "Why do we *want* to be good."

This struck me so hard because I, too, have come to this

10

point in my own, very different, struggles. I have long assumed that free will is an illusion and have worked hard to live without it, but doing this provokes a simple fear—what if I behave terribly badly? What if I give up all moral values and do terrible things? What indeed are moral values and how can I make moral decisions if there's no one inside who is responsible? I'm sure I don't need to go on. I suspect that this natural fear is the main reason why so few people sincerely try to live without free will. Like my Dad, they want to be good, and fear that if they stop believing in a self who chooses to do the right thing then they will run amok and all hell will break loose.

Is the fear justified? I suspect not.

Evolutionary psychology provides reasons why we want to be good, such as nurturing instincts shaped by kin selection, and the desire to earn brownie points in the game of reciprocal altruism; memetics provides other reasons, showing how altruistic *memes* (units of cultural information transferable from one mind to another) can spread so successfully; and most of us have been trained since early childhood to behave at least reasonably decently.

So it may just come naturally to us to want to be good, even though we so often fail. If this is true, this common fear is no excuse to carry on living in delusion.

Arguably, some of our most cruel and selfish behavior is caused, or at least exacerbated, by clinging to a false sense of an inner self who has consciousness and free will, in which case we might even behave better, rather than worse, if we could throw off the illusion. So it is by no means obvious that giving up believing in free will must be morally dangerous.

Another deep seated fear is that we will fail to do anything at all, and lose all motivation.

I have frequently had students who thought this way, "Why would I ever get up in the morning?" they ask.

I suggest they try the exercise and see what happens. What happens is that they lie there and get bored. Then they need to go to the loo, and once in the bathroom it seems nicer to have a shower and clean their teeth than go back to bed. Then they get hungry. And so the day goes on and things get done. In fact, if you keep practicing this way it becomes increasingly obvious that the physical body you once thought you inhabited does not need a driver or a ghostly supervisor. Distributed through its multiple parallel systems are the instincts, memories, control systems and skills of a lifetime that will ensure its coordinated actions and appropriate responses. It really is okay to trust in the universe and in one's own spontaneous actions. Then the feeling of free will simply loses its power.

My dad stopped at his question about goodness. Many people cannot accept his answer and want to go further. But in my experience—and I've asked many scientists and philosophers, as well as my own students—most intellectually reject the reality of free will while carrying on their lives "as if" it exists.

Indeed, I have often been told that it's impossible to live one's life without the illusion, and that everyone who lives happily and sanely must live "as if" they are free.

Whether you agree with them or not, you will find this

little book packed with exciting and challenging thoughts on free will, from some of the greatest minds of our time. Read it right through, or dip into it when you feel the illusion of free will creeping over you, and I'm sure you'll enjoy it as much as I have.

—Susan Blackmore, Ph.D.

"Deeds are done, events happen,
but there is no
individual doer thereof."

—BUDDHA

Introduction

You're about to embark on an exciting journey. You'll be reading about a subject that few people ponder privately or discuss publicly. You'll be jumping out of the mainstream mindset and into the lofty thoughts of more than fifty of the world's leading intellectuals.

Most people believe free will is special and important, yet define it simplistically. They say, "I have free will because I choose things." Choosing equals free will. This popular notion and others will be explored in chapter one.

Free will is an esoteric topic that mainly concerns philosophers and neuroscientists. I'm not a philosopher or a brain scientist, although I studied philosophy and many of the biological sciences at UCLA and Northwestern. So why did I become so infatuated with free will?

Four years ago, I was introduced to the concept of "non-doership" (no free will) by Ramesh Balsekar, an Advaita Vedanta teacher from Mumbai who gave daily satsang talks to traveling seekers.

"What are you seeking?" he asked his visitors.

"We want enlightenment, nirvana, to be lifted into a transcendent state in which there is no suffering, desire or pesky sense-of-self." A tall order, but Ramesh could fill it.

"Self-realization or enlightenment is nothing more than the deepest understanding that there is no individual *doer* or any actions, neither yours or anyone else's," he said. "You are not the thinker of any thoughts, nor the experiencer of any experiences. They just happen."

I eagerly absorbed Ramesh's books and tapes, then a nagging question obsessed me: *What do the world's leading scholars have to say about free will?* What if he's wrong, has been drinking too much chai and sniffing too much incense and sitting in the lotus position too long.

Next, I went on a research binge, shifted my focus from Indian gurus to Starbucks, where I read a pile of philosophy books on free will, mostly from Oxford University Press. I studied them ravenously and, as time passed, found several non-philosophy books and magazine articles about my arcane subject. I felt like Dr. Livingstone, bushwhacking through a jungle.

I sought opinions both for and against free will, but found no credible evidence in favor of it. (I didn't include theists in my quest.) A few scholars argued: "Yes, free will is a myth, but let's not tell the public. The truth might send them on a hedonistic rampage, might produce more cheaters and fewer cooperators. The time isn't right." But the majority disagreed: "Hey, people can live happily and morally without dodging the truth. Let's move forward."

The Myth of Free Will features a unique collection of authors who maintain that science can help us understand why free will is an illusion. It includes short essays (mostly excerpts), which are the gems of my research. You are reading the third edition, which is a revised, more polished version of the previous two editions. All three editions were produced for busy people who like to read in short bursts.

What are my qualifications for tackling such a daunting subject? My only qualification is that I'm a truth-seeker, a lover of reality. That's it! In fact, if I had passed away ten years ago, this book would not have materialized because I had no interest in free will and assumed I had it. My writing career would have ended with the publishing of my book *30 Days to a Simpler Life*.

I'll do my best to convince you that, since you never had free will, you have nothing to lose. That won't be easy because this old myth is compelling, flattering and widely accepted—and our culture of individualism fosters it. We are taught to take pride in being first causes or little gods.

Free will tells us we have a supernatural power. No wonder we adore it and base our lives on it.

Reading contrary information about free will takes guts because this myth is a big part of our personal identities. So as you read the essays and quotes, you may feel a bit woozy, like the rug has been pulled out from under you. Such feelings are natural. Expect them.

In the final chapter, I talk about the many benefits I have received from comprehending the truth about free will. I didn't expect to receive so many insights and wake-up calls, but have gladly invited them into my life.

If I do my job well, you will deeply understand why free will has such a firm grip on you and why giving it up, or downplaying it in your life, is a worthy pursuit.

As you read, ask yourself, *Who would I be without my belief in free will?*

1.

"I choose,
therefore I have free will."

When things turn out well,
we say we have free will.
When they turn out badly,
we say it's our destiny.

M ost people believe they have free will because they choose things. But choosing, as you will soon see, does not equal free will. Nonetheless, choosing is a very real human experience, and we do it trillions of times a day, consciously and (mostly) unconsciously.

Our choices propel us from one place to another, enable us to get our needs met, create our unique lives. Choosing is what humans do best. What follows is a brief description of The Choosing Process:

♦ *Options arise and we imagine outcomes.*
We consider the costs and consequences of our actions, wondering which option will bring us the most pleasure and least pain. We have many possible futures and that's exciting.

♦ *We select one, or more, options.*

As one option becomes stronger and more desirable than the others, we make a choice. Our emotions and reasons guide us.

♦ *We act on our choice.*

We act immediately or in the future. Of course, we can change our minds and abandon a project before it takes off. For example, we may select a fabulous restaurant and then decide to stay home and munch on popcorn while watching an award-winning foreign film such as "After the Wedding."

♦ *We judge the results.*

We often reflect on the outcome of our actions, a uniquely human ability. We think about how closely it matches our hopes, wishes and expectations.

It's not just choosing that convinces us we have free will, but the entire choosing process. Each step enhances our belief in this magical power.

"My soul is the chooser."

Many people believe they have a "soul/spirit" that directs their brain's decision-making circuitry. But what does this entity look like? My friend Tessa says, "My spirit is a translucent, glowing swirl of haze floating within and around my brain. It's made of energy and leaves my body when I die." She has described a supernatural agent.

But how does a nonphysical spirit communicate with a physical body part? How does it control decision making? And where is the Central Soul Bank? People who are seduced by this concept sidestep these relevant questions. What follows is dialogue from Scott Adams's book *God's Debris,* which brings this point home.

> "So where is free will?" he asked again.
> "It must involve the soul." I didn't have a better answer.
> "Soul? Where is the soul located?"
> "It's not located anywhere. It just is."
> "Then the soul is not physical in nature, according to you," he said.
> "I guess not. Otherwise someone probably would have found physical evidence of it," I said.
> "So you believe that the soul, which is *not* physical, can influence the brain, which is physical?"

Most reputable scientists say the soul, like free will and immortality, is a myth. For an illuminating book on the soul, read Owen Flanagan's *The Problem of the Soul: Two Visions of Mind and How to Reconcile Them.*

Perhaps you don't believe in souls, but still think that something directs your brain. Maybe you call it "the self" or "the ego" or an executive "I." If you think this way, you are a dualist, dividing the mind and brain into two different things. In reality, there is only one thing: the brain.

"Oh my gosh, my brain is the chooser!"

Your brain, that lump of jelly in your head that consumes roughly 20 percent of your body's energy, 23 percent of its calories, and 40 percent of its glucose, controls your choices—and it's fully capable of doing the job. It can juggle your competing options and select one, without the guidance of a paranormal assistant. What follows is a crash course on how your brain chooses:

In short, your brain's decision-making circuitry, in your frontal lobes, controls your choices. When you choose between a papaya and a banana, patterns of neural activity representing these two possibilities appear in your prefrontal cortex. Copies of each pattern grow and spread at different rates, depending on your past experiences and sensory impressions. Eventually, the number of copies of one pattern passes a threshold and you pick the papaya or banana—or buy the Honda or Toyota, or travel to Paris or Barcelona.

Decision-making spurs a battle in the brain. Two or more desires fight for supremacy. And the brain, because it must conserve its energy, frequently chooses a habit to quell the debate. Habits often bring maximum pleasure and minimum pain, give us a feeling of certainty that ends the cacophony.

Choosing is an extremely complex, cerebral event. Our brains store millions of emotional memories of past decisions and these memories drive our choices, too. "I continue to be fascinated by the fact that feelings are not just the shady side of reason, but that they help us reach decisions as well," says Antonio Damasio, professor of neuroscience at USC.

"Even the most mundane choices emerge as a vigorous debate," writes Jonah Lehrer in *How We Decide*. "Let's say that you're contemplating breakfast cereals in the supermarket. Each option activates a subset of competing thoughts. Perhaps, the organic is delicious but too expensive, or the whole-grain flakes are healthy but too unappetizing, or the Fruit Loops are appealing but too sugary. Each distinct claim triggers a particular set of emotions and associations, all of which compete for your conscious attention."

"Decision-making is a competition, a dynamic process in which there are winners and losers. The losers are never eliminated, but stick around to try and win again," says Alain Berthoz in *Emotion & Reason*. "Suppressed actions are always poised for a comeback." Mark Twain puts it this way: "When there are two desires in a man's heart, he has no choice between the two, but must obey the strongest, there being no such thing as free will in the composition of any human that ever lived."

"What's the role of my genes and past experiences?"

Contrary to popular self-help books, you can't become anyone you want to be. Everyone has a limited range of options, but that range keeps us plenty busy. We don't need more things to do.

Your unique options are determined by your *heredity* (genes) and *environment* (conditioning) and their complex interaction in your brain. Encoded in your DNA are your sex, race, appearance, personality, and more. Your conditioning includes what you learned from your parents, schooling, culture, social status, generation, and historical time-slot— all of your past experiences. Accepting that your choices are prompted by your genes, environment, and brain state does not diminish you in any way.

At any given moment, every action you perform is a result of your brain's interpretation of data. It may be hard for you to accept that your brain has the power to create and weigh your options and then guide your actions. Maybe you would rather believe that your brain is not powerful enough to control your choices and needs a supernatural soul to take charge. It's easy to fall into this trap because most decision-making is unconscious, and the human imagination easily congers up entities to explain the mysterious.

"But, I could've done it differently."

True, you can improve upon your performance the next time you're in a similar situation, but you can never repeat the past. You can't do the same tango twice, eat the same dessert, or have sex exactly the same way (though it may seem like it). What you do always reflects your strongest, most passionate desire. You are constantly manifesting what you want, whether you think so or not. And, in any instant, there is only *one* physically possible future.

Our strongest desire wins because it has the greatest chance of being satisfied and bringing us the most pleasure. We choose the option that makes us feel the best at the time. Usually, a creaky habit captures our attention because it's an activity that works for us on many levels.

Still, we can do things in a variety of ways, even though we are constrained by our genes, environment, and brain state. Our options are wild and varied.

Of course, sometimes we look back and think, "I wish I'd done it differently." That's called "regret" and we are wired for it. Regret helps us improve our performances—and sometimes it makes us crazy.

Finally, there is another reason why you couldn't have done it differently. I read about it in Dr. Read Montague's fascinating book, *Why Choose This Book: How We Make Decisions*. He's a professor in the department of neuroscience at the Baylor College of Medicine as well as a fellow at the Institute for Advanced Studies in Princeton.

It's about your values...

"The sneaky secret about choice is that it's not about choice at all—it's about values," says Montague. "The act of choosing one action over another follows directly from the way the brain values both the external world and the internal world—our thoughts. And the surprise about valuation is that it arose because life runs on batteries and so decisions must be efficient. Value and efficiency."

He says that every choice comes with an *energy-rating tag* to keep the brain from blowing a circuit. The secret is, our

24

values are related to energy conservation. "From its humble beginnings, life discovered subtle mechanisms of efficient valuations and embedded them in the human brain. It's the mechanism that constrains our choices, anchoring them firmly to our biological needs. Choices are not magic, descending from some immaterial place like cost-free manna."

This idea still has me reeling. There is so much to learn and grasp about the brain. Writing this book has changed my mantra from "Know thyself" to "Know thy brain."

"Still, it feels as if I have free will."

We *all* feel like we have free will. Deeply understanding that free will is a myth and illusion need not strip you of that comfy, inborn, blissful feeling of being a "me," having a sense of self that separates you from others. But it is possible to let go of the fantasy and, at the same time, enjoy the feeling. Why not savor the evolved feeling of free will as you would a performance by magicians such as Houdini, James Randi, Penn and Teller, and David Copperfield?

From an evolutionary perspective, a feeling of free will (strong self-centeredness) helped our species survive and reproduce, but now we are mature enough to become semi-detached from the illusion and appreciate it for what it is.

But why bother, you ask? Because our survival in this high-tech world depends on our being honest with ourselves, on understanding who we really are, our true nature. In primitive societies, illusions and pseudoscience had benefits. Today is different and the stakes are much higher. I like what Arnell Dowret, the producer of "Equal Time for Free Thought," has to say about our inborn feeling of free agency:

"Although our everyday experiences make us feel as if free will exists, unless they are looked at objectively, they will give us a faulty understanding of ourselves. Carl Sagan was fond of saying, 'Extraordinary claims require extraordinary proof.' It is clear that the claim that we have free will *because we feel as if we do* doesn't come close to meeting this stringent requirement."

As I was preparing to send this book to the publisher, my friend Randy called and sounded a bit miffed.

"I've lived my whole life trusting in free will and it sounds like you're telling me to drop it."

"Actually, I'm not," I said. "I don't think you should try to drop it. Instead, I'd like you to become familiar with the evidence against it and the downside of the myth, then lose interest in it, *or not.* Just go with the flow."

He said he felt relieved, less coerced, that I was detached, which I am. He got that I'm not into arm-bending, but into sharing, educating, and making a difference.

Likewise, my wish is that you deeply absorb the material in this book and truly understand why free will is a myth, and don't try to drop it. Just join me on this journey.

2.

The Myth & Causality

Men believe themselves to have free will
because they are conscious of their actions,
and unconscious of the causes
whereby those actions are determined.

—BARUCH SPINOZA

Everything that happens has a cause. Everything you think, say and do occurs because something preceded it. Nothing can appear without being brought about, created, or formed by antecedents or precursors.

Moreover, every effect becomes a cause. Effects don't just dangle aimlessly, loll about and play hooky. They deftly, and oftentimes swiftly, prod other things into action. They are powerful instigators. "Cause and effect are two sides of one fact," said Ralph Waldo Emerson.

To identify causes, ask, "Why did this happen?" To identify effects, ask, "What happened because of this?" The following is an example of one cause producing one effect:

Cause: You are out of gas.
Effect: Your car won't start.

Sometimes, many causes contribute to a single effect or many effects may result from a single cause. The realization that our behavior is produced by impersonal causes enables us to take ourselves and others less seriously.

Albert Einstein said, "Scientific research can reduce superstition by encouraging people to think and view things in terms of cause and effect."

Our ignorance of "causal chains" leads us to believe in free will.

A causal chain is a series of causes leading to an effect. We cannot know *all* of the causes of our choices in any one chain, but we can know the effect and a few obvious causes. Our ignorance of hidden causes tricks us into thinking we have free will. Here are three kinds of causes.

- ◆ *Accessible Causes*: Causes we can know. We can readily spot a few causes for a recent event. "I parked too close to that black truck and scraped my door."

- ◆ *Hidden Causes*: Causes we can't know. Most of these happened before we were born, like the impact on your life of the sack of Rome.

- ◆ *False Causes*: Causes that are just plain wrong. We often make up causes when we try to understand people's motivations. "She did it because..." We can be totally off-base and not know it. (Causes are often indistinguishable from reasons.)

HOMEWORK: Watch the films *Matchpoint, City Island,* and *Run Lola Run* to observe dramatic causal chains.

We think of ourselves as first causes, prime movers or little gods.

What would it be like to actually have free will? For starters, you would be able to sidestep your brain's programming. You would be able to act without being influenced by your genes and conditioning. What would life in this bizarre lane look like? Here's my take on it:

With free will, you would flounder in a tumultuous sea of "What shall I do next? I can't make up my mind." As a first cause, you would become paralyzed with indecision, confusion, and purposelessness. With your clever genes and past experiences squelched, you would become rudderless. Your life would have no meaning.

Welcome to inertia, lying in a recliner without even a beer and pretzels. And you thought that giving up your belief in the myth would lead to an existential meltdown. Truly having free will would take you there much faster.

Okay, so you've got that, but what about determinism? What's that all about? And why should you care?

The notion of cause-and-effect is related to the idea of "determinism."

The *Stanford Encyclopedia of Philosophy* defines determinism as "the idea that every event is necessitated by antecedent events and conditions together with the laws of nature."

Sounds like an expansion of what we've been saying in the previous sections about cause-and-effect.

Many people tell me that determinism is the same as fatalism, the harsh, depressing and false idea that no matter what we do, the future will turn out a particular way. Our actions often make all the difference in the world in how things turn out. Nor is our behavior perfectly predictable or inevitable. It's sometimes outrageously quirky.

And then there's "indeterminism," or the doctrine that *not all events* are determined by prior causes, that our will is to some extent independent of motives. Indeterminism suggests to some people that humans have free will, that we can ignore our genes and past experiences, and totally wing it.

As you read the short essays that follow, pay attention to these words: *causes, causation, causality, contra-causal, causal chains, determined, determinants,* and *determinism.*

Keep in mind, the essays are brief because this book was designed for a mainstream audience. It's also for people who know that free will is a myth (the choir) and want to share this understanding with friends who don't have the time or inclination to wade through scholarly texts, and who would rather watch a 20-minute TED video lecture on a computer or read a newspaper on an e-book or sail to Tahiti. In other words, it's a guide for the casually curious.

Why Are YOU
Reading This Book?

BY DANIEL WEGNER

Dan is a professor of psychology at Harvard University and the author of The Illusion of Conscious Will, *required reading for anyone interested in free will. It is less philosophical than empirical, drawing heavily on recent research in cognitive science and neurobiology.*

So, here you are reading a book on free will. How could this have happened? One way to explain it would be to examine the causes of your behavior.

A team of scientific psychologists could study your reported thoughts, emotions, and motives, your genetics and your history of learning, your social situation and culture, your memories, physiology and neuroanatomy, and lots of other things. If they had access to all of the data they could ever want, the assumption of psychology is that they could uncover the mechanism that gives rise to all your behavior and so could explain why you picked up this book at this moment. However, another way to explain the fact of your reading this book is to say you decided to pick it up and begin reading. You freely willed what you are doing. You have a kind of personal power, an ability to do what you want when you want.

These *two explanations* are both appealing but in different ways. The scientific explanation accounts for behavior as a machine and appeals to that part of us that knows how useful science is for understanding the world. It would be wonderful if we could understand people in just the same way.

The free will explanation has a much deeper grip on our intuition. It feels more right. Why? Because we each experience ourselves willing our actions many times a day. *We feel that we cause ourselves to behave.*

The idea of free will and the idea of a psychological mechanism have an oil and water relationship, having never been properly reconciled. One way to put them together is to say that the mechanistic approach is the explanation that is preferred for scientific purposes, but a person's experience of free will must be understood scientifically as well.

The mechanisms underlying the experience of will are themselves a topic for study. We should be able to examine and understand what creates the experience of will and what makes it go away.

This means, though, that free will is an illusion. It is an illusion in the sense that *the experience of consciously willing an action is not a direct indication that the conscious thought has caused the action.*

Dr. Wegner's Myth-Busters

• We experience a walk in the park, winding a clock, or smiling at someone, and the feeling keeps our notions of ourselves as persons intact. But our sense of being a free agent who does things comes at a cost of being technically wrong all of the time.

• Sometimes how things seem is more important than what they are. This is true in theater, in art, in used car sales, in economics, and—it now turns out—in the scientific analysis of free will. It seems we have minds. It seems we are free agents. It seems we cause what we do. Although it is sobering and ultimately accurate to call all this an illusion, it's a mistake to conclude that the illusory is trivial.

• We can't possibly know (let alone keep track of) the tremendous number of mechanical influences on our behavior because we inhabit an extraordinarily complex machine. So we develop a shorthand, a belief in the causal efficacy of our conscious thoughts. We believe in the magic of our own causal agency.

• If the mind can make us "experience" an airplane, why couldn't it produce an experience of *itself* that leads us to think that it causes its own actions. The mind creates this continuous illusion. It really doesn't *know* what causes its own actions.

• Free will in an illusion, but it's a very persistent illusion—it keeps coming back. It's like a magician's trick that's been seen again and again. Even though you know it's a trick, you get fooled every time.

The Ghost in the Machine

BY STEVEN PINKER

Steve is a Professor of Psychology at Harvard University having previously been the director of the Center for Cognitive Neuroscience at MIT. In his book, The Stuff of Thought, *he asks about what language tells us about how we think. He says the words and grammar we use reflect inherited rules that govern our emotions and social relationships.*

In the traditional view of "The Ghost in the Machine," our bodies are inhabited by a self or soul that chooses the behavior to be executed by the body. These choices are not compelled by some prior physical event, like one billiard ball smacking into another and sending it into a corner pocket.

The idea that our behavior is caused by the physiological activity of a genetically-shaped brain refutes the traditional view. It makes our behavior an automatic consequence of molecules in motion and leaves no room for an uncaused chooser.

One fear of determinism is a gaping existential anxiety: that deep down we are not in control of our own choices. All of our brooding and agonizing over the right things to do is pointless, it would seem, because everything has already been preordained by the state of our brains.

If you suffer from this anxiety, I suggest the following experiment: For the next two days, don't bother deliberating over your actions. It's a waste of time; they have already been determined. Shoot from the hip, live for the moment, and if it feels good do it. No, I am not seriously suggesting that you try this! But a moment's reflection on what would happen *if you did* try to give up making decisions should serve as a Valium for your anxiety.

The experience of choosing is not a fiction, regardless of how the brain works. It is a real neural process, with the obvious function of selecting behavior according to its foreseeable consequences. It responds to information from the senses, including the warnings of other people. You cannot step outside it or let it go on without you, because it is you.

Dr. Pinker's Points

• If scientists wanted to show that people had free will, what would they look for? Some random neural event that the rest of the brain amplifies into a signal triggering behavior? But a random event does not fit the concept of free will any more than a lawful one does.

• Everything we do is an evolutionary adaptation designed to carry out a major function. The illusion of free will falls into this category.

• Science is guaranteed to chip away at the concept of free will because the scientific mode of explanation cannot accommodate the mysterious notion of *uncaused causation* that underlies the will.

• Scientists have not exorcised the ghost from the machine because they are killjoys, but because they have amassed evidence that every aspect of consciousness can be tied to the brain.

• People naturally believe in "The Ghost in the Machine," that we have bodies made of matter plus spirits made of an ethereal something. Yes, people acknowledge that the brain is involved in mental life. But they still think of it as a pocket PC for the soul, managing information at the behest of a ghostly user. Modern science has shown that there is no user. The "soul" is, in fact, the information processing activity of the brain. New imaging techniques have tied every thought and emotion to neural activity.

• In this scientific age, to understand behavior is to explain it as a complex interaction among (1) the genes, (2) the anatomy of the brain, (3) its biochemical state, (4) the person's family upbringing, (5) the way society has treated him or her, and (6) the stimuli that impinge upon the person.

• The Bottom Line: Thoughts and thinking are no longer ghostly enigmas but mechanical processes that can be studied, and the strengths and weaknesses of different theories can be examined and debated.

"The mind is determined to wish
for this or that by a cause, which has
also been determined by another cause,
and this again by another, and so on
to infinity. This realization teaches us
to hate no one, to despise no one,
to mock no one, to be angry
with no one, and to envy no one."

Baruch Spinoza

(November 24, 1632 - February 21, 1677)

Nothing to Fear

BY ARNELL DOWRET

Arnell is a freethought activist, writer, and facilitator of "Secular Connections," an alternative, experiential workshop for freethinkers. He is the associate producer and a host of the WBAI radio program "Equal Time for Freethought" in New York City. Arnell is a contributing author to Toward a New Political Humanism, *Prometheus Press, 2004. His current project is a book presenting Naturalism as a radical, alternative "spiritual path."*

Our universe appears to be governed by the laws of cause-and-effect and human behavior is no exception to this rule. There exists no legitimate evidence for anything which accounts for the way we behave other than the complex combination of our genes and how they interact with our environment.

Despite this, the idea that our behaviors are the inescapable result of causes seems to contradict and undermine the ways in which we experience ourselves and the behaviors of others.

Turn Right or Left?

When we make everyday choices, such as turning right or left, we certainly feel as if we are free to defy even our own expectations. So if, at the very last second, we decide to turn left instead of right, we would probably feel we had asserted our free will, unaffected by any outside influence.

But even as we make that last minute decision, we are still acting according to our determinants. Like every other moment in time, the moment immediately preceding our decision to turn left instead of right is connected to, and results from, the moment immediately preceding it, just as that preceding moment, is connected to and results from all of the moments preceding it. For this reason every decision we make reflects the entire history of our genes and the way they have interacted with our environment to make us the persons we are.

The Two Brothers

It's also common to have known people who outwardly seem to have had identical determinants yet greatly vary in the manner in which they behave. Imagine two biological brothers, raised by the same parents, in the same home, educated at the same schools, and exposed to the same social groups—yet their lives take vastly divergent trajectories such as one brother becoming a successful and praised member of society while the other seems to fail at everything.

Rather than proving the existence of free will, the example of the two brothers demonstrates how the genetic and environmental determinants that shape us can be so numerous, complex, and subtle that they can and frequently do elude predictability; but unpredictable does not mean without cause. Although accurate prediction of the weather can sometimes be elusive, only the most primitive of minds would conclude that the weather must therefore be driven by its own free will.

Putting Up a Wall

For many people the mere suggestion that human behavior is fully caused, and not chosen, can result in them *putting up a wall* that greatly reduces their abilities to hear anything further on the subject; they will protest that were it not for the belief in freewill, people would be paralyzed with a sense of abject futility, society would be plunged into immorality and chaos, and life would seem pointless. *Such fears are baseless.*

Understanding that our lives are driven by determinants does not persuade anyone to be less productive or moral than they would have been before gaining such an understanding. There is no intellectual understanding that can negate our need to act upon our world—we're compelled to act as we do because, like all other living things, we are compelled to seek pleasure.

If we are fortunate enough to have had determinants in our lives which motivate us to improve our own lives as well as the lives of others, we will do so because it feels good; it doesn't matter that what motivates our behavior are factors that we did not choose. If we are lucky enough to find ourselves engaged in the process of living in a satisfying and productive way, we will not suddenly be happy staying in bed and not functioning, or at least not for very long.

For those who are not functioning very well, believing in free will is unlikely to lead to high-level achievement. In contrast, because most people who experience difficulty functioning will often also suffer with low self-esteem, understanding that their behavior is the result of determinants and not the result of their own free will can be of significant value. To recognize that one's personal problems are not because of one's own inherent worthlessness, sinfulness, laziness, evil, or any of the numerous labels which our society uses to blame people for having difficulties, but are instead the consequence of determinants, determinants which would compromise the ability to excel of even the most well-functioning of individuals. *This is a major step toward self acceptance, personal growth, and greater accomplishment.*

Path of Least Resistance

No matter how some behaviors may seem to imply the contrary, like water running down a hillside, behaviors will always follow the path of least resistance. In animal and human terms, it means we do what feels good and avoid doing what is painful. No matter how much a particular behavior seems to be an example of an individual choosing the "hard way" over the "easy way," or making a sacrifice for the good of someone else, all living things including humans, act in accordance with their determinants.

Those who are programmed by their determinants to pull over in the rain and help a stranded motorist jump start their car, while certainly performing an act of kindness, would find the experience of passing the stranded motorist to be more uncomfortable than the disturbance of stopping to help.

People who are driven to help others and contribute to our world are fortunate to have had determinants which support their healthy behavior and enable them to experience feeling potent, connected to their world, and have the satisfying sense that they can make a difference; their behavior is not the result of virtuous choice, it's the result of their determinants.

Understanding that it's our determinants that make us who we are, as opposed to the magical belief in free will, would also result in our becoming a healthier society.

The more that our society accepted the decisive role which our determinants play in shaping our behavior, the more we would become effective at establishing an environment which supported people's emotional health, and strengthened their sense of connection to each other.

In such a society, socially desirable behaviors would become more prominent than behaviors that are anti-social, and personal satisfaction and pride would occur when one person is helpful to another, rather than when one successfully manages to convince another to purchase their stock at an inflated price.

Additionally, a society which accepted the truth of our determined behavior would not be vulnerable to those who behaved antisocially; although such a society would reject solutions which were retributive or vindictive, its far more accurate understanding of the factors which influence behavior would enable it to be considerably more effective at protecting its citizens than societies which believed in free will.

Going to the Movies

To those who fear that the acceptance that human behavior is determined would make life seem pointless, consider that when we go to see a movie or read a book, it doesn't matter that the story's outcome is already decided. The point of going to a movie or reading a book is not to find out the story's ending—that could usually be learned by simply reading the review. Instead, the real reason we read a book or go to a movie is to experience the way the story unfolds, with all of its surprising twists and turns. It's from this that our pleasure is derived.

In reality, even though all that happens is fully determined, we can never be entirely aware of all of the determinants involved, and consequently can never be completely sure of what will happen next. We are left with the experience of participating in a story whose outcome cannot be predicted, and like a movie, with the real pleasure derived from watching the story unfold.

Understanding the decisions we make as being the result of determinants provides a perspective on life that is both amazing and elegant. That there is continuity of cause-and-effect in the cosmos, and that our everyday actions reflects that continuity, is a far more splendid and satisfying interpretation of human behavior than the illogical and disjointed notion that from somewhere inside of us emanate actions which have no cause.

To be conscious of our inexorable connection to the infinite chain of cause and effect, which preceded and will follow our brief moment of existence, is profoundly humbling. When we observe our fellow human behaving in ways we can not understand, it beckons us to acknowledge that—"There but for those determinants go I." It teaches us that the "ends" hardly matter as much as do our means of achieving them; that our "journey there" is really all there is.

In essence, the most important wisdom, which we might hope to attain from any traditional "spiritual path," is embodied in the naturalistic truth that human behavior, like everything else in our classical universe, is fully determined and free will is just an illusion.

Objections to Determinism

The main reasons why people reject the idea that our behaviors are determined (caused), and not the result of free will, fall into two categories:

1. Determinism is not intuitive—it feels as if we really do have free will.

The truth of determinism is hard to perceive if our understanding is solely based on our everyday experiences and intuitions, because these can lead us to erroneous conclusions.

2. People fear that accepting determinism would bring dreadful consequences.

The fear of dire consequences resulting from accepting our lack of free will is unfounded. Recognizing how determinants play out in our lives is satisfying and empowering.

The Paradox of "Feeling Free" in a Determined Universe

BY MICHAEL SHERMER

Michael is the founding publisher of Skeptic *magazine and a columnist for* Scientific American. *His essay invites you to think about numbers, how many causes it takes to bring about an action.*

Scholars of considerable intellectual power for many millennia have failed to resolve the paradox of feeling free in a determined universe. One provisional solution is to think of the universe as so complex that the number of causes and the complexity of their interactions make the predetermination of human action pragmatically impossible.

We can even put a figure on *the causal net* of the universe to see just how absurd it is to think we can get our minds around it fully.

It has been computed that in order for a computer in the far future of the universe to resurrect in a virtual reality every person who ever lived or could have lived, with all causal interactions between themselves and their environment, it would need 10 to the power of 10 to the power of 123 bits (a 1 followed by 10^{123} zeros) of memory. Suffice it to say that no computer within the conceivable future will achieve this level of power; likewise no human brain even comes close.

The enormity of this complexity leads us to feel as if we are acting freely as uncaused causers, even though we are actually causally determined. Since no set of causes we select as the determiners of human action can be complete, *the feeling of freedom arises out of this ignorance of causes*. To that extent we may act "as if" we have free will.

More about Michael

Few can talk with more personal authority about the range of human beliefs than Michael Shermer. At various times in the past, he has believed in fundamentalist Christianity, alien abductions, Ayn Rand, and megavitamin therapy. Now he believes in skepticism and critical thinking.

Michael is the author of *The Science of Good and Evil: Why People Cheat, Gossip, Care, Share, and Follow the Golden Rule* and *Why People Believe Weird Things: Pseudoscience, Superstition, and Other Confusions of Our Time*. Check out his awesome website at www.Skeptic.com.

46

Freedom Evolved

BY DANIEL C. DENNETT

Dan is a Professor of Philosophy at Tufts University. He is best known for his arguments that free will boils down to physical processes. So in his essay below, this means he isn't talking about the contra-causal free will of the soul, but a free will compatible with determinism.

The *idea* that we have free will is a background condition for our whole way of thinking about our lives. We count on it. We count on people "having free will," the same way we count on them falling when pushed off cliffs and needing food and water to live. Free will is like the air we breathe, and it's present almost everywhere we want to go, but it's not only not eternal, it evolved, and is still evolving.

The atmosphere of our planet evolved over hundreds of millions of years as a product of the activities of simple early life-forms, and it (the illusion) continues to evolve today in response to the activities of the billions of more complex life-forms it made possible.

The atmosphere of free will is the enveloping, enabling, life-shaping, *conceptual* atmosphere of intentional action: planning, hoping, promising, honoring, blaming, resenting, and punishing.

We all grow up in this *conceptual* atmosphere, and we learn to conduct our lives in the terms that it provides.

It *appears to be* as stable, as eternal and unchanging as arithmetic, but it is not.

The idea that we have free will evolved as a recent product of human interactions, and some of the kinds of human activity it first made possible on this planet may also threaten to disrupt its future stability, or even hasten its demise. Our planet's atmosphere is not guaranteed to last forever, and neither is our concept of free will.

Dr. Dennett's Determinism

• We have more freedom if determinism is true than if it isn't. Because if determinism is true, then *there is less randomness*. There's less unpredictability. To have freedom, you need the capacity to make reliable judgments about what's going to happen next, so you can base your actions on it.

• Free will is not what tradition declares it to be: a God-like power to exempt oneself from the causal fabric of the physical world. It is an evolved creation of human activity and beliefs, and it is just as real as such other human creations as music and money.

• One widespread tradition has it that we human beings are responsible agents, captains of our fate, *because* what we really are are *souls*, immaterial and immortal clumps of Godstuff that inhabit and control our material bodies rather like spectral puppeteers. It is our souls that are the source of all meaning and the locus of all our suffering, our joy, our glory and shame. But this idea of immaterial souls, capable of defying the laws of physics, has outlived its credibility thanks to the advance of natural sciences.

The Princeton Soul Poll

BY LEE M. SILVER

Lee holds a Ph.D. in Biophysics from Harvard University and is a professor of Molecular Biology at Princeton University. His book, Challenging Nature: The Clash of Science and Spirituality at the New Frontiers of Life, *takes a fresh look at the collision of science, religion, pseudoscience, and politics.*

The conviction that human beings are endowed with free will is pervasive, even more so than a belief in the human soul. In my anonymous survey of 335 randomly chosen undergraduates at Princeton, 78 percent expressed confidence in the existence of free will, while only 53 percent were confident about an immaterial human spirit. (Students could answer "yes," "no," and "I am not sure what I think.")

Most dramatic was the difference in responses from male and female students. Of the 173 women surveyed, only three (compared with 19 out of 162 men) were confident enough in their personal convictions to answer "no" to the existence of free will.

A spirit or soul are terms for an imagined physical entity that controls physical objects. According to Owen Flanagan, a philosopher and popular author, a belief in free will serves as a "quick and reliable diagnostic test" for an implicit belief in some kind of soul because "the only device ever invented that can do this sort of job (expressing free will) is an incorporeal soul or spirit." And yet remarkably, a quarter of the students at Princeton have faith in free will at the same time they claim to reject the existence of immaterial human spirits.

Chaos Theory

Many people think that free will is the only alternative to a deterministic view of human mentality. But an understanding of brain biology, quantum mechanics, and chaos theory indicates otherwise. Together, the trillions of neurons in your brain make trillions of individual "firing decisions" every day. And at the threshold between a choice to fire and not, the addition or subtraction of a single neurotransmitter molecule, even a single electron, will sometimes make a difference. Intuitively, it might seem that the choice made by a single neuron couldn't possible have a significant effect on a brain composed of trillions of other neurons. But in the late twentieth century, with the development of *chaos theory*, scientists discovered that tiny changes can stimulate an entire pathway of brain activity leading to one mental state rather than another.

Dr. Silver's Sterling Remarks

• In the early twentieth century, many philosophers and psychologists who dismissed the existence of free will came to the conclusion that consciousness, feelings, imaginings, and a subjective inner "self" must be an illusion as well.

• As a philosophical concept, free will is like an *onion* whose skin has been completely peeled away—and at its core, it ceases to exist.

"Our actions should be based on
the ever-present awareness that humans
in their thinking, feeling and acting
are not free, but are as *causally bound*
as the stars in their motion."

—ALBERT EINSTEIN

Quotes on Causality

"The universe is a gigantic clockwork mechanism, slavishly unfolding according to deterministic laws. How then does a free agent act? There is simply no room in this *causally closed system* for an immaterial mind to bend the paths of atoms without coming into contact with physical laws. Nor does the famed indeterminacy of quantum mechanics help minds to gain purchase on the material world."
—**Paul Davies,** *The Mind of God*

"The first dogma which I came to disbelieve was that of free will. It seemed to me that all notions of matter were *determined* by the laws of physics and could not be influenced by human wills." —**Bertrand Russell,** *philosopher*

"To what extent do animals have causal beliefs—that is, beliefs about what causes movement and events in the world around them? The answer is rather little. It is causal understanding that makes us human."
—**Lewis Wolpert,** *Six Impossible Things Before Breakfast*

"I act as though I were a free agent, but when an action is performed, it is clear that all the forces of the universe conspired to *cause* it." —**Somerset Maugham**

"Our behavior is not random, so it must have a *cause*. And if behavior has a cause, it must not be free."
—**Matt Ridley,** *Nature Via Nurture*

"The universe is a network of causation, of which you are one insignificant node, yet one that would be difficult to replicate." —**V. S. Ramachandran,** *neuroscientist UCSD*

"I've yet to discover a single interpretation of *genetic determinism* that carries any of the implications people seem to worry so much about. On the contrary, it turns out that whatever applies to genes applies equally to environments. So if people fear genetic determinism, they should be worrying equally about *environmental determinism*."

—**Helena Cronin,** *philosopher*

"Give me the choice between my actions being strict *causal outcomes* of my genes, my history, my personality, the state of my mind/brain, and the current environment, and I will take that, every day of the week, over the view that when I deliberate or act, I do so randomly, because my will has flown the *causal* coop."

—**Owen Flanagan,** *The Problem of the Soul*

"Cause and effect, means and ends, seed and fruit cannot be severed; for the effect already blooms in the *cause*, the end pre-exists in the means, the fruit in the seed."

—**Ralph Waldo Emerson**

"The general delusion about free will is obvious, because man has power of action, & he can seldom analyze his motives (originally mostly *instinctive*, & therefore now great effort of reason to discover them...) he thinks they have none."   —**Charles Darwin,** *Notebooks*

"The vast majority of persons experience a 'feeling' of free will when making a choice, like choosing vanilla ice cream over chocolate. For them, making choices proves a person has free will. No proof could be more obvious. But are choices ever completely free? That question we can answer easily: All human choices are constrained by many *causes*."

—**William B. Provine,** *Cornell professor*

3.

The Myth & Morality

Moral decisions are complex,
involving the interplay of thought and emotion,
as well as anguish and ambivalence.

As neuroscientists peer deeper into our brain, they are discovering more and more genes and brain structures for feelings like empathy, disgust, and joy. That is, they are finding that we are hardwired for morality, that there are physical bases for the feelings that create moral behavior.

Morality would not exist without two broad regions of the brain: the emotional brain and the frontal lobes. "Within these regions are three faculties that compose the elite machinery geared toward facilitating social interaction and maintaining order through social morality: the amygdala, the inhibitory networks (mainly the anterior cingulate cortex, hippocampus and hypothalamus) and the prefrontal cortex (mirror-neuron system)," says Laurence Tancredi in *Hardwired Morality.*

We think of moral decisions as warring internal desires. But most of the time, we actually decide whether an action is right or wrong *automatically.* Our moral intuitions are similar to our aesthetic judgments: we instantly know what we think is beautiful or ugly.

Marc Hauser, author of *The Moral Mind*, says, "Some moral judgments arise like flashes of lightening—spontaneous, unpredictable, and powerful. Other judgments emerge slowly and deliberately, alighting after carefully weighing the pros and cons of each option." So what are some ways humans behave morally without much prompting? Why are we so good most of the time?

♦ **Kinfolk Goodness:** The lives of relatives are felt to be more valuable than those of strangers. If a house in on fire and your only son is locked in one bedroom and three unrelated children are locked in another, which bedroom would you go to if you only had time for one? Most people would choose their own child over the other three. This is called "kin altruism."

♦ **Back-Scratchin' Goodness:** It pays to be generous to others if they can be counted on to be generous in return. I'll scratch your back, if you'll scratch mine. This is called "reciprocal altruism."

♦ **In-Your-Face Goodness:** We are kinder to people who are nearby. A weeping child evokes more sympathy than thousands of impoverished people in foreign countries: *Out of sight, out of mind.* But why are we so calloused? Our hunter-gatherer ancestors didn't spend time with people who lived in far away valleys, and we inherited their brains, which are wired for proximity. Never mind that today we wear Chinese clothes and eat French cheeses.

♦ **Similarity Goodness:** Many studies show that we are nicer to people who resemble us—look like us, dress like us, speak like us and share our beliefs.

The Role of Mirror Neurons

Mirror neurons, located in the motor cortex, enable us to sympathize with others. When someone cries, groans, yawns, or smirks, we tune into their minds, feel what they feel.

"Mirror neurons underwrite our ability to recognize what helps or distresses others, what they suffer and enjoy, what they need and what harms them. This means that the ultimate basis for moral judgment is hardwired—and therefore universal. So even when customs differ, fundamental morality does not," says A. C. Grayling, Professor of Philosophy at the University of London.

Moral Chimpanzees

Most people believe that only humans will assist strangers without receiving anything in return, sometimes at a great personal cost to themselves. Here's an excerpt from *Science News* (June 30, 2007) that explains why chimpanzees also belong to the Good Samaritan Club.

> Without any prospect of immediate benefits, chimps helped both people and other chimps they didn't know, says Feliz Warneken of the Max Planck Institute for Evolutionary Anthropology. The roots of human altruism reach back roughly six million years to a common ancestor of people and chimps. "Learning and experience are also involved in altru-

istic helping, but our claim is that there is a predisposition in chimps and people to develop such behavior without training," he says.

Two Kinds of Responsibility

There's *ultimate responsibility* and *proximate responsibility*. Humans are ultimately not responsible for their actions because they don't have free will. Proximately, however, we can be held responsible (accountable) for our actions, for disobeying the laws of the lands we inhabit and pass through. Accountability teaches us to behave ethically in a civilized society. So don't worry that responsibility will vanish when humans understand that free will is an illusion.

In short, the proximate/ultimate distinction enables us to understand how we can be both responsible and not responsible. At first this notion befuddled me. After a while, the two kinds of responsibility sunk in.

Genes & Criminal Law

The mind-boggling advancements in genetics are jeopardizing the free will foundation upon which the criminal justice system is based. Justifications for punishment that rely on individual blame are becoming tough to justify because of the infinite causes of every human action. Many legal scholars understand this, only too well, and fear that the American criminal justice system will implode if its foundation in free will is shattered. Perhaps these nervous scholars underestimate the resiliency of the criminal justice system. Nonetheless, maintaining our social order is crucial.

Here's what attorney Matthew Jones wrote in the *Duke Law Journal* (2003): "Genetic discoveries will alter the vision of what it means to participate in criminal justice. The core acceptance of free will and the corresponding dependence on individual responsibility will no longer be embraced in American criminal jurisprudence. It is only the utilitarian theory of punishment that can survive the implications of genetic findings, while still providing a system that allows for the maintenance of societal order and showcasing the human need to see individual suffering. American criminal jurisprudence will thus focus less on the individual and more on the greater society in evaluating various modes of punishment. It is this radical reformulation as to the very reason society punishes individuals that will be the true long-term effect of the genetic revolution on criminal law."

Morality Is Partly Situational

Philip Zimbardo, professor emeritus of psychology at Stanford University, author of *The Lucifer Effect*, says, "How can moral people be seduced to act immorally? Where is the line separating good and evil, and who is in danger of crossing it? In my book, I attempt to understand and deal with the fundamental question, *What makes people go wrong?* But instead of resorting to a traditional religious dualism of good versus evil, of wholesome nature versus corrupting nature, I look at real people engaged in life's daily tasks, surviving within an often turbulent crucible of human nature. I seek to understand the transformations of their character when they are faced with powerful *situational forces*."

Improving Parenting

"Free will is the bottom line excuse for social policies, which perpetuate the cycle of crime and punishment. If we believe criminality arises from individuals' freely-willed choices, its actual biological, social and economic causes will go unexplored and unaddressed. The myth lets us off the hook. When we come to appreciate the causal story behind crime, we'll seek to *prevent* crime instead of punishing it after the fact. True, it is individuals who commit offenses and they must be dealt with, compassionately and effectively. But the reasons they become offenders lie in the conditions that created them, so we must hold *society* responsible—ourselves, our families, schools and communities, as well as the offenders—in our quest for a safe, flourishing culture," writes Thomas W. Clark in *Encountering Naturalism.*

Antisocial and criminal behavior tends to run in families, but scientists weren't sure whether this was due mostly to environmental factors or biological ones. It turns out both play a role, but the effect is more dramatic when they act together. This has been illustrated in several studies over the past six years which found that male victims of child abuse are several times as likely to become criminals as abusers themselves if they were born with a less-active version of a gene for the enzyme "monoamine oxidase A" (MAO-A), which breaks down neurotransmitters crucial to the regulation of aggression. Indeed, the cost to society of failing to intervene in abusive homes is bound to breed greater problems than the cost of improving parenting.

Basil Fawlty's Car

BY RICHARD DAWKINS

Richard is the Charles Simonyi Professor of the Public Understanding of Science at Oxford University and the author of The God Delusion *and* The Greatest Show on Earth.

B asil Fawlty, British television's hotelier from hell created by the immortal John Cleese, was at the end of his tether when his car broke down and wouldn't start. He gave it fair warning, counted to three, gave it one more chance, and then acted.

"Right! I warned you. You've had this coming to you!"

He got out of the car, seized a tree branch and set about thrashing the car within an inch of its life. Of course, we laugh at his irrationality.

Instead of beating the car, we would investigate the problem. Is the carburetor flooded? Are the sparking plugs or distributor points damp? Has it simply run out of gas?

Why do we not react in the same way to a defective man: a murderer, say, or a rapist?

Why don't we laugh at a judge who punishes a criminal, just as heartily as we laugh at Basil Fawlty? Or at King Xerxes who, in 480 BC, sentenced the rough sea to 300 lashes for wrecking his bridge of ships?

Isn't the murderer or the rapist just a machine with a defective component? Or a defective upbringing? Defective education? Defective genes?

Dr. Dawkins's Take on Crime

• Doesn't a truly scientific, mechanistic view of the nervous system make nonsense of the very idea of [ultimate] *responsibility*? Any crime, however heinous, is in principle to be blamed on antecedent conditions acting through the accused's physiology, heredity and environment.

• Is retribution as a moral principle compatible with a scientific view of human behavior? As scientists, we believe that human brains, though they may not work in the same way as man-made computers, are as surely governed by the laws of physics. When a computer malfunctions, we do not punish it. We track down the problem and fix it, usually by replacing a damaged component, either in hardware or software.

Hume's Fork
Either our actions are determined,
in which case we are not responsible for them,
or they are the result of random events,
in which case we are not responsible for them.

—Oxford Dictionary of Philosophy

Mouse Rap

BY TAMLER SOMMERS

Tamler received his Ph.D. in Philosophy at Duke University and is Assistant Professor of Philosophy at the University of Houston. He is researching morality across cultures.

Imagine for a moment that instead of Timothy McVeigh destroying the Murrah Federal Building in Oklahoma City, it had been a mouse. Suppose this mouse got into the wiring of the electrical system, tangled the circuits and caused a big fire, killing all those inside. Now think of the victims' families.

There would, of course, still be enormous grief and suffering, but there would be one significant difference: There would no resentment, no consuming anger, no hatred, no need to see the perpetrator punished (even if the mouse somehow got out of the building) in order to experience "closure." *Why the difference?*

Because McVeigh, we think, committed this terrible act out of his own free will. He chose to do it, and he could have chosen not to. McVeigh, then, is morally responsible for the death of the victims in a way that the mouse would not be. And our sense of justice demands that he pay for this crime.

There is an undeniable human tendency to see ourselves as free and morally responsible beings. But there's a problem.

We also believe—most of us anyhow—that our environment and our heredity entirely shape our characters. (What else could?) But we aren't responsible for our environment, and we aren't responsible for our heredity. So we aren't responsible for our characters. But then how can we be responsible for acts that arise from our characters?

There's a simple but extremely unpopular answer to this question: *We aren't.* We are not and cannot be ultimately responsible for our behavior. According to this argument, while it may be of great pragmatic value to hold people responsible for their actions, and to employ systems of reward and punishment, no one is really deserving of blame or praise for anything.

Tamler's Remarks

• In order to have free will and ultimate responsibility, we would have to be self-caused, and this is logically impossible.

• Perhaps Spinoza and Darwin are right—that the primary reason we believe ourselves to have free will is that we are *aware* of the desires and volitions that cause our actions, but *unaware* of what causes the desires and volitions themselves.

To Go Deeper

Read Tamler's book, *A Very Bad Wizard: Morality Behind The Curtain,* essential reading for anyone interested in profound insights into human morality. He interviews ten acclaimed researchers in the burgeoning field of moral psychology. Questions he asks: Does free will exist? What counts as justice in the Peruvian rainforest? Does evolutionary theory make ethics a sham?

Strawberry or Chocolate?

BY LAURENCE TANCREDI

Laurence is a psychiatrist-lawyer and Clinical Professor of Psychiatry at the New York University School of Medicine.

We go into an ice cream parlor and choose a chocolate sundae over a strawberry sundae. It is a seemingly simply choice, and we claim that our taste preference has dictated it. Yet choices are never that simple.

The choice of chocolate is influenced not only by taste, but also by color, texture, presentation—and more than likely by earlier pleasant memories associated with flavor. Nonetheless, the decision about ice cream is simple compared to decisions about which strategy to select to solve a complex math problem, or to personal choices like whether to leave one's job for one that pays less but might provide more opportunity for advancement—or for one that is more fulfilling though is might pay less and offer little opportunity for advancement.

Choices of any complexity always involve layers of multifaceted mental (brain) activity, and often many interrelated decisions.

But neuroscience is forcing us to rethink the extent of our personal control over our choices, and the implications of the limits on personal control over our choices are nothing short of mind-boggling. Imagine that free will, long regarded as a hallmark of the human condition, may not be an untrammeled quality.

Imagine that we are not quite as "free" as we would wish—and that biological forces produced by genes and the environment may be more powerful than anyone every believed possible in influencing an individual's decisions.

Gambling Addicts

The issue of "responsibility" is compelling when we talk about gambling. Some people are in complete control; they can take or leave the gambling experience. Toward the other end of the spectrum are the problem gamblers on the verge of addiction, with the capacity for considerable risk-taking but little control over their habit. Then, finally, come the pathological gamblers, clearly addicted and impulsive. For both the problem gambler and the pathological one, control and power over one's behavior is an issue.

The implications of the degrees of lack of control over monetary decisions and gambling as they impact on individual decisions are far reaching. They call into question the person's ability to exert *free will* and self-determination, and therefore his or her responsibility for engaging in an immoral act. The evidence is strong that the way we treat money depends to a great extent on the nature and degree of our brain's hardwiring.

Dr. Tancredi Says

• Social morality begins in the brain, for without the brain, there would be no concept of morality.

• A long line of studies have shown that males lie nearly two to three times more often than females and that their primary objective is to promote themselves. Women, on the other hand, lie primarily for self-protection. They may lie about a variety of things, such as how they spend their day, how they feel about their partners, and medical reasons for not having sex.

• *Being moral isn't easy.* This is why moral training—early and often—is essential. Our brain structures aren't immutable. They are susceptible to change for the better and change for the worse. What's important is what happens deep down at the level of the neuron in a process called *neuroplasticity.* By neuroplasticity we mean the ability of neurons at the synapses to forge new connections, thereby essentially bringing about a rewiring of the brain.

• Going down the dangerous route with drugs, gambling, sex, or others addictions is a matter of neuroplasticity. What often starts off an innocent experiment—drinking alcohol, or smoking pot—can develop over time into compulsive, addictive behavior. The brain changes, adapts because new circuitry, and includes more and more bad behavior.

• The more complex our choice, the more we are fortified in our conviction of ownership and self-determination.

To Delve Deeper

In his book, *Hardwired Behavior: What Neuroscience Reveals about Morality*, Laurence updates and sharpens the debate between biology and blameworthiness by examining the latest findings in neuroscience. You will be challenged to rethink your ideas about free will and responsibility.

Goodbye Retribution, Yes!

BY WILLIAM B. PROVINE

William is a professor at the Cornell University, Department of Ecology and Evolutionary Biology.

From the perspective of evolutionary biology, organisms are locally determined by heredity and environment, and their interaction. Thus no organism can have free will, and indeed the idea of free will is unintelligible. Humans, however, widely believe in a myth of free will.

The question is, do we benefit enough from this myth to justify basing our lives on it? Is the usual philosophical dictum that belief in "free agency" is required for moral responsibility answer enough? Without moral responsibility, societies become bestial and individuals are overcome by nihilism and disillusionment. So say the philosophers.

Does the myth of free will have negative social consequences? Yes, and they are huge. Blame, revenge, and retribution dominate modern society, from personal relationships to between countries.

Evil consequences so outweigh the benefits of belief in the myth of free will that, even if we really did have it, we should pretend we don't.

I have concluded that free will is entirely disconnected from moral responsibility. When an individual behaves well in society, she exhibits her past experiences, education, and training, but no free will. Humans can live well without free will, and escape entirely nihilism and disillusionment.

Human society free of this myth would be kinder and more caring than our present societies.

Using free will as an excuse we condone a vicious attitude of revenge toward anyone who does wrong in our society. Most of the movies in a video store are based upon getting even with some nasty person. This attitude leads to a grossly expensive and hopeless system of punishment in America, though much of the same attitude can be found in most countries around the world.

Without the free will myth, justification for revenge disappears and rehabilitation becomes the main job of judicial systems and prisons. We will all live in a better society when this myth is dispelled.

Tit-for-Tat

Blame alone is a serious downside of belief in free will. It, however, is the least destructive downside of free will. Usually, when someone is offended by the behavior of someone else, after blame comes the strong desire to get even with the offender. This response is known the world over as tit-for-tat, or an "eye for an eye" or "tooth for a tooth." Getting even is a restrained response to offense. You are doing nothing more to the other personal than he did to you. But surely it goes beyond blame.

Even the restrained response of getting even with a social offender can lead to lots of human misery. The famous feuds between the Hatfields and the McCoys near Harlan, Kentucky, or killing back and forth between Israelis and Palestinians, or between Catholics and Protestants in Ireland, are based explicitly on getting even for past mis-

deeds. Once these feuds begin, ending them is always difficult because neither side feels that they are even, but behind.
Lesser feuds dominate work and home life. When folks are
bent on getting even with others nearby, the quality of life
for all involved goes down.

Dr. Provine's Points to Ponder

• What a relief to me to discover that humans have no such
thing as free will. I agree 100-percent with Einstein about
the benefits of having no free will. If someone insists on
blaming me, then I diminish the relationship to a manage-
able level instead of worrying about getting even.

• Since the great majority of people on earth believe they
have free will, and consider it important, would an understanding that they actually had no free will at all be a major
blow?

> *What is the self of self-control?*
> *The brain constructs a range of*
> *make-sense-of-the-world neurotools.*
> *One is the future, one it the past,*
> *and one is the "self." So, in essence,*
> *the self is a construction of the brain*
> *—a real, but brain-dependent*
> *organizational network. It's a bit like*
> *a utility on your computer.*

—PATRICIA CHURCHLAND
Professor of Philosophy, UCSD

Are Sinners Merely Poorly Calibrated Clockwork?

BY SAM HARRIS

Sam is a graduate in philosophy from Stanford University. For 20 years, he has studied Eastern and Western religious traditions. Read his latest book, The Moral Landscape: How Science Can Determine Human Values.

Free will is an illusion in that it cannot even be rendered coherent *conceptually*, since no one has ever described a manner in which mental and physical events could arise that would attest to its existence. Surely, most illusions are made of sterner stuff than this. If, for instance, a man believes that his dental fillings are receiving radio broadcasts, or that his sister has been replaced by an alien who looks exactly like her, we have no difficulty specifying what would have to be true of the world for his beliefs to be true. Strangely, our notion of free will achieves no such intelligibility. As a concept, it simply has no descriptive or logical moorings.

The belief that human beings are endowed with free will underwrites both our religious conception of "sin" and our judicial ideal of "retributive justice." Without free will, sinners would just be poorly calibrated clockwork, and any notion of justice that emphasized their punishment (rather than rehabilitation or mere containment) would seem deeply incongruous. Happily, we will find that we need no illusions about a person's place in the *causal order* to hold him accountable for his actions. We can find secure foundations for ethics and the rule of law without succumbing to illusions.

The idea of free will is an ancient artifact of philosophy as well as a subject of occasional, if guilty, interest among scientists. Despite the clever exertions of many philosophers who have sought to render free will "compatible" with deterministic accounts of mind and brain, the project seems hopeless.

The endurance of free will, as a problem in need of analysis, is attributable to the fact that most of us feel that we freely author our own actions (however difficult it may be to make sense of this notion in logical or scientific terms).

What most people overlook is that the concept of free will does not correspond to any subjective fact about us. Consequently, even rigorous introspection soon grows as hostile to the idea of free will as the equations of physics have, because apparent acts of volition merely arise, spontaneously and cannot be traced to point of origin in the stream of consciousness.

Say It Again Sam

• A moment or two of self-scrutiny and the reader might observe that he no more authors the next thought he thinks than the next thought I write.

• Iron Age beliefs about God, the soul, sin, and free will continue to impede medical research and distort public policy.

Fat Teens Sue McDonald's

BY CLAY SHIRKY

Clay is the adjunct professor at the Graduate School of the Interactive Telecommunications Program, New York University, and the author of Here Comes Everybody: The Power of Organizing without Organizations.

Free will is going away. It's time to redesign society to take that into account. In 2002, a group of teenagers sued McDonald's for making them fat. They claimed that the corporation used promotional techniques to get them to eat more than they should. The suit was condemned as an the erosion of the sense of free will and personal responsibility in our society. Less widely remarked upon was that the teens were offering an accurate account of human behavior.

Consider the phenomenon of super-sizing, where a restaurant patron is offered the chance to increase the portion size of their meal for some small amount of money. This presents a problem for the concept of free will. The patron has already made a calculation about the amount of money they are willing to pay in return for a particular amount of food. However, when the question is re-asked—not "Would you pay $5.79 for this total amount of food?" but "Would you pay an additional 30 cents for more French fries?" Patrons often say yes, despite having answered "No" moments before to an economically identical question.

Super-sizing is designed to subvert conscious judgment, and it works. By re-framing the question, fast food companies have found ways to take advantages of weaknesses in our analytical apparatus, weaknesses that are being documented daily in behavioral economics and evolutionary psychology.

This matters for more than just fat teenagers. Our legal, political, and economic systems all assume that people are uniformly capable of consciously retraining their behaviors. As a result, we regard decisions they make as being valid and hold them responsible for actions they take, as in contract law or criminal trials. Then, in order to get around the fact that some people obviously aren't capable of controlling their behavior, we carve out exemptions. In U.S. criminal law, a 15 year old who commits a crime is treated differently than a 16 year old. A crime committed in the heat of the moment is treated specially. Some actions are not crimes because their perpetrator is judged mentally incapable, whether through developmental disabilities or other forms of legally defined insanity.

This theoretical divide, between the mass of people with a uniform amount of free will and a small set of exceptional individuals, has been broadly stable for centuries, in part because it was based on ignorance. As long as we were unable to locate any biological source of free will, treating the mass of people as if each of them had the same degree of control over their lives made perfect sense. However, today that notion of free will is being eroded as our understanding of the biological causes of behavior improves.

Criminal law is just one area where our concept of free will is eroding:

- ♦ We know that men make more aggressive decisions after they have been shown pictures of attractive female faces.
- ♦ We know women are more likely to commit infidelity on days they are fertile.
- ♦ We know that patients committing involuntary physical actions routinely (and incorrectly) report that they decided to undertake those actions to preserve their feeling of control.
- ♦ We know people will drive across town to save $10 on a $50 appliance, but not on a $25,000 car.
- ♦ We know that the design of the ballot affects a voter's choices.

In the coming decades, our concept of free will, based as it is now on ignorance of its actual mechanisms, will be destroyed by what we learn about the actual workings of the brain. We can wait for that collision, and decide what to do then, or we can begin thinking through what sort of legal, political, and economic systems we need in a world where our old concept of free will is rendered inoperable.

www.jolyon.co.uk

Living Happily & Morally

BY SUSAN BLACKMORE

Sue is a Senior Lecturer in Psychology at the University of the West of England, Bristol. She has a degree in psychology and physiology from Oxford University.

It is possible to live happily and morally without believing in free will. As Samuel Johnson said: "All theory is against the freedom of the will, and all experience is for it."

With recent developments in neuroscience and theories of consciousness, theory is even more against it than it was in his time, more than 200 years ago. So I long ago set about systematically changing the experience. I now have no feeling of acting with free will, although the feeling took many years to ebb away.

But what happens? People say I'm lying! They say it's impossible and so I must be deluding myself to preserve my theory. And what can I do or say to challenge them? I have no idea—other than to suggest that other people try the exercise, demanding as it is.

When the feeling is gone, decisions just happen with no sense of anyone making them, but then a new question arises—will the decisions be morally acceptable? Here, I have made a great leap of faith: It seems that when people throw out the illusion of an inner self who acts, as many mystics and Buddhist practitioners have done, they generally do behave in ways that we think of as moral or good. So perhaps giving up free will is not as dangerous as it sounds.

As for giving up the sense of an inner conscious self altogether—this is very much harder. I just keep on seeming to exist. But though I cannot prove it—I think it is true that I don't.

Sue's Books on Consciousness

Sue is the author of *Ten Zen Questions* and *Conversations on Consciousness: What the Best Minds Think about the Brain, Free Will, and What It Means to Be Human*. In the latter, she asks Caltech Professor Christof Koch, "How do you cope with believing that free will does not exist?" He replies, "Free will in the metaphysical sense really implies there's action without any physical precedents. Now as scientists, or even as a thinking person, we know that can't be the case. There always have to be physical precedents [causes]. So I only mean I am free in the sense that it's not you who is determining my actions—it's not blind force. My actions are determined by my genes, upbringing, predilections, and desires. All of this, plus some random component depending on fluctuation and noise in my brain, comes together in making a decision one way or the other way."

* The copyrighted illustration was created by Sue's artist son Jolyon at jolyon.co.uk.

Quotes on Morality

"I don't believe in free will. Schopenhauer's words, *Man can do what he wants, but he cannot will what he wants*, accompany me in all situations throughout my life and reconcile me with the actions of others, even if they are rather painful to me. This awareness of the lack of free will keeps me from taking myself and my fellow men too seriously as acting and deciding individuals, and from losing my temper."

—**Albert Einstein,** *My Credo*

"No one can be *ultimately* deserving of praise or blame for anything. It's not possible. This is very, very hard to swallow. Ultimately, it comes down to *luck*: Luck, good or bad, in being born the way we are. Luck, good or bad, in what then happens to shape us. We can't be buck-stopping responsible for what we do, and at the same time, it seems we can't help believing that we do have absolute responsibility."

—**Galen Strawson,** *philosopher*

"Perhaps the idea of free will is a cultural phenomenon. If so, we must not assign blame to people for personal failures, we should instead understand the larger system and its influence on the individual."

—**Heidi Ravven,** *philosopher*

"Everybody happily, gratefully, applies the Golden Rule when it comes to interacting with the famous. Thou must treat the famous as thou wouldst wish to be treated thyself. Easy! If only everybody could be famous, we would all be effortlessly altruistic."

—**Rebecca Newberger Goldstein,**
30 Arguments for the Existence of God

"We evolved a moral instinct, a capacity that grows naturally within each child, designed to generate rapid judgments about what is morally right or wrong based on an unconscious grammar of action. Part of this machinery was designed by the blind hand of Darwinian selection millions of years before our species evolved; other parts were added or upgraded over the evolutionary history of our species."

—**Marc Hauser,** *Moral Minds*

"Free will may be an illusion, but responsibility and moral action is quite real."

—**Daniel Wegner,** *Professor of Psychology at Harvard*

"When a man acts in ways that annoy us, we wish to think him wicked. We refuse to face the fact that his annoying behavior is the result of antecedent causes which, if you follow them long enough, will take you beyond the moment of his birth, and therefore to events for which he can't be held responsible by any stretch of imagination. When a motorcar fails to start, we don't attribute its annoying behavior to sin. We don't say, you are a wicked motorcar and can't have any more gasoline until you go."

—**Bertrand Russell,** *philosopher*

"In failing circumstances, no man can be relied on to keep his integrity." —**Ralph Waldo Emerson**

"When man studies himself with honest impartiality, he observes that he is not the voluntary artisan of his feelings or of his thoughts, and that his feelings and his thoughts are only phenomena which happen to him."

—**Hubert Benoit**
Zen & the Psychology of Transformation

"FREE WILL? -- I THINK THEY NEED MORE *STRUCTURE* THAN THAT."

"The biology of consciousness offers a sounder basis for morality than the unprovable dogma of the immortal soul."

—**Steven Pinker,** *Professor of Psychology at Harvard*

"The ethical and moral systems that emerge out of traditional religious and political systems frequently have common views on *right and wrong.* But perhaps the reason they do is that, in our species, the mind has a core set of reactions to life's challenges, and that we attribute a morality to these after the fact."

—**Michael Gazzaniga,** *The Ethical Brain*

"Once you understand someone's behavior on a sufficiently mechanical level, it's very hard to look at them as evil. You can look at them as dangerous; you can pity them; but evil doesn't exist on a neuronal level."

—**Joshua D. Greene**
Assistant Professor of Psychology at Harvard

"The trouble with statistics is they don't activate our moral emotions. Depressing numbers [of needy people] leave us cold: our mind can't comprehend suffering on a massive scale. This is why we are riveted when one child falls down a well, but turn a blind eye to millions of people who die every year for lack of clean water. Or why we donate thousands of dollars to help a single African war orphan featured on the cover of a magazine."

—**Jonah Lehrer,** from his blog *The Frontal Cortex*

"If one were to choose one single event in our daily living that is the most common, it would perhaps be the fact that in almost any group of people, the subject of the conversation is about someone being blamed—someone is responsible, someone should be punished.

"Blaming has become the very basis of living and has been causing the suffering which the Buddha considered the essence of life. He therefore concluded that the only way to end this suffering was to accept that 'Events happen, deeds are done, but there is no individual doer thereof.'

"The arising of a thought is spontaneous. Anything, of course, can happen, but a thought that is likely to occur to a doctor is not likely to occur to a lawyer or a mechanic. The thought that occurs in a particular human has to do with its natural characteristics. The thought about the equation that arose in Einstein's brain could not have occurred in anyone else's. Each individual human is created with certain characteristics, so that certain actions will take place. These actions are part of the impersonal functioning of Totality [nature]. Everything is happening according to Cosmic Law. No one is to blame for anything."

—**Ramesh S. Balsekar,** *Advaita Vedanta master*

4.

The Myth & the Brain

Of course, the mind is a product of the brain.
How could it not be?

—Eric R. Kandel, neuroscientist

Most people think the mind and brain are two separate things. Debating if this is true or false is often called the mind-body problem. What follows are four similar stances on the problem by scholars who agree that the mind and brain can't be split into two things.

Antonio Damasio, author of *Looking for Spinoza,* says, "The mind-body problem splits the mind to one side and the body and its brain to the other. This view is no longer mainstream in science or philosophy, although it is probably the view that most humans today regard as their own."

Paul Bloom, author of *Descartes Baby*, says the likelihood that a separate mind exists is highly improbable. "The mind is what the brain does, and so every mental event, from falling in love to worrying about our taxes, is going to show up as a brain event. In fact, if one were to find an aspect of thought that did not correspond to a brain event, it would be the discovery of the century."

Henry D. Schlinger, psychology professor, says, "The term 'mind' is sometimes used synonymously with the term 'brain,' which causes confusion by having two words for the same thing. In my view, if one believes that mind and brain are the same thing, then the term 'brain,' should be used because it avoids all of the metaphysical pitfalls associated with discussions of non-physical entities."

P. Z. Myers, biologist, University of Minnesota, and creator of the blog *Pharyngula*, puts it this way: "The mind is clearly a product of the brain, and the old notions of souls and spirits are looking increasingly ludicrous, yet these are nearly universal ideas, all tangled up in people's rationalizations for an afterlife, for ultimate reward and punishment, and their concept of self...If people continue to object to the lack of exceptionalism in our history, if they're resistant to the idea that human identity emerges gradually during development, they're most definitely going to find the idea of soullessness and mind as a byproduct of nervous activity horrifying...Our challenge as humans is to accommodate a new view of ourselves and our place in the universe that isn't encumbered with falsehoods and trivializing myths. We're in the midst of an ongoing revision of our understanding of what it means to be human—we are struggling to redefine humanity, and it's going to radically influence our future."

So scientists say that the mind is a brain activity and not a separate entity. How many of the world's best minds need to state this fact before believers in duality opt for reality?

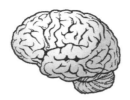

The Astonishing Hypothesis

BY V. S. RAMACHANDRAN

Rama is a neuroscientist and Director of the Center for Brain and Cognition at the University of California, San Diego. He is the author of A Brief Tour of Human Consciousness *and* The Tell-Tale Brain.

What Francis Crick referred to as "the astonishing hypothesis" is the notion that our conscious experience and sense of self is based entirely on the activity of a hundred billion bits of jelly, the neurons that constitute the brain. We take this for granted in these enlightened times, but even so it never ceases to amaze me.

Some scholars have criticized Crick's tongue-in-cheek phrase on the grounds that the hypothesis he refers to is "neither astonishing nor a hypothesis." (Since we already know it to be true.) Yet the far-reaching philosophical, moral and ethical dilemmas posed by his hypothesis have not been recognized widely enough.

Let's put this in historical perspective. Freud once pointed out that the history of ideas in the last few centuries has been punctuated by "revolutions"—major upheavals of thought that has forever altered our view of ourselves and our place in the cosmos. First, there was the Copernican system dethroning the earth as the center of the cosmos. Second, was the Darwinian revolution; the idea that far from being the climax of *intelligent design* we are merely neotonous apes that happen to be slightly cleverer than our cousins. Third, the Freudian view that even though you claim to be "in charge" of your life, your behavior is in fact governed by a cauldron of drives and motives of which you are largely unconscious. Fourth, the discovery of DNA and the genetic code with its implication (to quote James Watson) that "There are only molecules. Everything else is sociology."

To this list we can now add the fifth, the "neuroscience revolution" and its corollary pointed out by Crick—the "astonishing hypothesis"—that even our loftiest thoughts and aspirations are mere by products of neural activity. We are nothing but a pack of neurons.

Rama's Self-Talk

• The "self" results from a dynamic interplay of signals from three sources: signals from the skin, muscles and gut; inhibitory signals from the prefrontal cortex; and input from mirror neurons. From this fluctuating mosaic of brain activity emerges your sense of an embodied self.

• Your sense of body ownership, and of being a distinct entity, seems to derive in part from a network of brain cells known as *mirror neurons*. Located in the premotor cortex, they interact with your prefrontal cortex, the part of the brain that makes plans and decisions. Ordinarily, when you move your hand to reach for a pen (a motion accompanied by a sense of having free will), certain motor-command neurons in the motor cortex fire.

Benjamin Libet's
CLASSIC STUDY

In the 1970s, Benjamin Libet wired people to an electroencephalogram and measured 1) when they reported having a particular conscious thought about an action, say by pushing a button, and 2) when the nerve impulses corresponding to the initiation of the action started.

Astoundingly, the latter came first: that is, subjects had actually made (unconsciously) the decision to act measurably earlier than when they became aware of it consciously.

The conscious awareness in a sense was a "story" that the higher cognitive parts of the brain told to account for the action. It's as if the conscious brain was not the decider but simply the spokesperson.

—MASSIMO PIGLUCCI
Free Inquiry magazine

16 Brain Biases

Cris Evatt—C'est moi!—is working on a book titled Brain Biases, *which will feature two-page descriptions of more than 100 hardwired, cognitive quirks. What follows are short summaries of a few biases she will tackle.*

We come into this world with a hidden repertoire of brain biases, unconscious prejudices that cause errors in our thinking and sabotage our intentions. By producing fast decisions and strong actions, these hardwired mental shortcuts were adaptive, enabled our ancestors to survive better in a hunter-gatherer world. Today, however, many of these nomadic inventions offer few, if any, benefits. As you read the summaries that follow, think about which biases are useless hand-me-downs and which are keepers.

Brain biases are forces that influence the decisions you make. They are hard to spot because they are subtle, mundane, hidden mechanisms. If you don't become highly aware of them, they can sneak up on you.

The biases cause serious errors in judgment because they press us to take action without deliberating. Fortunately, not all of the biases are worthless. Many are useful, clever, and even humorous. As you read this section, ask yourself, "Does this bias benefit me or undermine my values? When it arises, should I let it be or let it go?"

LOSS-AVERSION BIAS

Finding losses roughly twice as painful as we find gains pleasurable.

When making decisions, people typically show a much greater sensitivity to losses than gains. "Loss aversion is now recognized as a powerful mental habit with widespread implications," writes Jonah Lehrer in *How We Decide*. "The desire to avoid anything that smacks of a loss often shapes our behavior. For example, loss aversion explains one of the most common investment mistakes: investors evaluating their stock portfolios are most likely to sell stocks that have increased in value. Unfortunately, this means that they end up holding on to their depreciating stocks. Over the long term, this strategy is exceedingly foolish, since ultimately it leads to a portfolio composed entirely of shares that are losing money."

Nations have lingered in wars and gone into debt because of loss aversion. Once a military establishment and government have committed time and money and innocent lives to a cause, it's hard to convince them it is futile and misguided. They refuse to admit they made a mistake. Viet Nam comes to mind.

In the late 1970s, Daniel Kahneman and Amos Tversky made waves when they demonstrated this bias. In 2007, UCLA scientists measured loss aversion in several brain regions, most notably in the prefrontal cortex and ventral striatum. Of all of the cognitive biases, this one seems to intrigue people the most. That's why I put it first.

OPTIMISM BIAS

Viewing ourselves as invulnerable
(or less likely than others)
to experiencing negative life events.

We are hardwired to expect pleasant outcomes in the future even when there is no evidence for them. People expect to live longer and be healthier than average. (I polled ten friends and all but two expect to live into their mid-eighties.) People underestimate their likelihood of getting divorced, yet the majority of first marriages crumble. People expect to complete personal projects, like building their dream house on the side of a cliff, in less time than it actually takes. And vacationers expect greater joy during upcoming trips than they actually experience.

Two new books, *Bright-Sided* by Barbara Ehrenreich and *Never Saw It Coming* by Karen Cerulo, ask us to consider optimism's downside, to grasp the brain's role in steering us away from potential problems: "The brain stores information in categories and the more an item fits the category ideal, the more precisely it is defined in the mind," writes Cerulo. "Because best-case examples of a concept are highly detailed, anything less than the ideal becomes increasingly nondescript. Because a concept's *worst-case scenarios* display minimal similarity to the category ideal, the brain routinely distances them from active consideration."

So it's a struggle for the brain to bring up bad scenarios because it consigns them to the fringes of consciousness. In other words, the brain won't take us there. It doesn't want to get into trouble.

ILLUSORY-CORRELATION BIAS

Inaccurately linking an action and an effect.

After a delightful birthday lunch at Poggio's in Sausalito, my friend Dawn, a fitness trainer who's hiked the 2,000 mile Pacific Coast Trail twice, and I went for a casual stroll in my hilly neighborhood.

Back at the house, she gasped, "Did you know your fingers are blue? You might not be getting enough oxygen to your extremities. Take off your shoes, let's see if your toes are blue, too."

They weren't, which baffled us even more. We talked about calling a doctor, but first I needed to go to the bathroom. While sitting on the john, I glanced down at my hands, which were resting on my new unwashed blue jeans.

"The jeans did it!" I screamed.

"No way."

"Let's see if it comes off," I said, lathering my hands with soap. Then I ran them across my white kitchen counter and, voila, it turned blue. We howled, realized we had been snookered by an illusory correlation.

According to David Ludden, associate professor of psychology at Lindsey Wilson College in Kentucky, there is a strong urge in humans to seek causes for events in their lives, and we fall for the ones we manufacture even if they're wrong. "No other species makes causal inferences like we do," says Ludden. " This ability clearly gave humans a strong evolutionary advantage, allowing them to understand and—and hence control—their environments to a greater degree than any other animal. Still, our ability to ascertain causality is not that reliable. For one thing, we are prone to causal illusions—we infer causal relationships where none exist. Furthermore, when we are unable to explain why events occur, we feel distressed, so we tend to make up explanations with little or no evidence to support them. Nevertheless, the advantages of this ability to construct beliefs about causal relationships must have outweighed the negative side effects for early humans."

So now I know why Dawn and I quickly fabricated a link between oxygen-deprivation and my fingers. What if we'd gone to the hospital? Would the doctors have figured out the true cause? Or would they have made up an illusory correlation, too?

My friend Lynn calls this bias "The Jumping-to-Conclusions Bias" because it appears instantly along with a feeling of certainty. (Read Dr. Robert Burton's book, *On Being Certain: Believing You're Right When You're Not*.)

BETTER-THAN-AVERAGE BIAS
Thinking we're better than average at many things.

People generally think they are smarter, luckier and better looking than they actually are. They regard themselves as exceptional and believe they will avoid the divorces, accidents, and premature deaths that strike and shock everyone else. Flawed self-assessment is common in our species. So why worry about falling for this one? Because unrealistic views of ourselves can endanger our health, ruin our relationships, and ruin our finances.

CONTRAST BIAS

Mentally upgrading or downgrading an object when comparing it to a contrasting object.

We are constantly comparing things, people and situations. Then we call them desirable or undesirable according to what we've recently experienced in the same category.

• A lifted weight is felt as heavier than normal when contrasted with a lighter weight. And it is perceived as lighter when compared with a heavier weight.

• A person appears more attractive when contrasted with a person who is less attractive and less attractive when contrasted with one who is more attractive.

DENIAL BIAS

Disbelieving an uncomfortable fact.

When there is overwhelming evidence and we reject it, we are in denial, a defense mechanism that shows up in several disguises. Here are six:

• **Denial of Fact:** Lying about facts to avoid the truth.

• **Denial of Responsibility:** Sidestepping responsibility by blaming, minimizing, or justifying.

• **Denial of Impact:** Not admitting to the harm one's actions have caused to oneself or others.

• **Denial of Awareness:** Claiming to be in an altered state of consciousness (livid, drunk, stoned, sleepy).

• **Denial of Cycle:** Avoiding seeing one's pattern of thinking and acting that led to an outcome.

• **Denial of Denial:** Saying, "But I'm not in denial."

BEAUTIFUL-PEOPLE BIAS

The tendency for attractive people to receive more rewards.

One day, Jenny and I were driving down the freeway when she saw a cop chatting with a sexy blonde. "She won't get a ticket because she's pretty," said Jenny, miffed, looking more like Kathy Bates than Kate Hudson. "I wonder how many times that woman has been given a break?"

Many studies have shown that attractive people get more advantages, effortlessly. For instance, attractive students get higher marks from professors, good-looking patients get more personalized care from doctors, and handsome criminals receive lighter sentences. Size matters, too. Tall people earn more money throughout their careers than their shorter co-workers. Also, overweight women are more likely to be unemployed than thin women.

Despite the fact that human beings are hardwired to respond more favorably to attractive people, anyone can become more appealing to others by acting cheerful, dressing well, listening attentively, and maintaining eye contact.

STATUS QUO BIAS

Wanting things to stay the same.

We get stuck in established behaviors unless the incentive to change is compelling. In the film "Yes Man," Jim Carrey stars as Carl Allen, a man who signs up for a self-help program based on one simple principle: *Say yes to everything and anything new.* Unleashing the power of "yes" changed Carl's life in wonderful and unexpected ways.

WISHFUL-THINKING BIAS

Wanting something to be true that is clearly false.

We often believe that if we wish hard enough for something, it will come true. We twist the facts. For example, if I believe I'm talking to my deceased Danish grandmother Mary, I'm engaged in wishful-thinking. There is no proof that she is present. (There may be evidence that I'm hallucinating.) Also called "The Tinkerbell Effect."

ANCHORING BIAS

Relying too heavily on one piece of information when making decisions.

During normal decision-making, we often anchor on one piece of information at the expense of more important data. We narrow our sights. Then once the anchor is set, there is a bias toward clinging to the information. For example, when my mother went boat-shopping, she focused excessively on the "cute" blue curtains of an older Chris-Craft, but didn't consider the engine. Ultimately, she paid $30,000 for a vessel that never left the slip.

OSTRICH EFFECT

Avoiding risky situations by pretending they don't exist.

Have you ever been told, "You've got your head in the sand?" The name of this bias comes from the legend that ostriches bury their heads in the sand to avoid danger. In behavioral economics, the ostrich effect is the avoidance of obvious risky financial situations by pretending they don't exist.

CONFIRMATION BIAS

Seeking evidence that agrees with our position and dismissing evidence that does not.

My husband Dave and I spent a year preparing for Y2K because we believed a computer glitch would bring down the world's power systems in one fell swoop. Instead of calmly listening to opposing views, we spent hours online looking for evidence to confirm our fears. We planted a garden, dried vegetables, stored water, installed solar panels, and formed a support group. All good stuff—for the wrong reason. We were overwhelmed by feelings of self-righteousness and thought the future would validate us. Today, I make an effort to seek opposing viewpoints, to think critically like Michael Shermer, editor of *Skeptic Magazine.*

INSTANT-GRATIFICATION BIAS

Minimizing the future and caving in to short-term highs.

Over millions of years, evolution selected strongly for creatures who lived largely in the moment. In every species that has ever been studied, animals tend to value the present far more than the future, and humans are no exception. When we're hungry, we gobble up that greasy pizza as if driven to lard up on carbs and fat now, since we might not find any tomorrow. Discounting the future also affects how we spend money, why we fail to save enough for retirement, and why we rack up credit card debt. We're hugely hardwired for shortsightedness.

SELF-SERVING BIAS

Taking credit for successes and blaming others, or situations, for failures.

An employee who receives a promotion might say, "I got promoted because I do excellent work," whereas an employee who doesn't get promoted might say, "I got passed over because my boss doesn't like me, is a jerk." We are motivated to protect our self-esteem, to come up with feel-good rationalizations. And we may not even believe our own stories (bullshit) but invent them to make a good impression on others.

GROUPTHINK BIAS

Doing and thinking things because others do.

We do many things in a group we wouldn't do alone. Group leaders mesmerize us. Group cohesion gets things done. We adopt group fears, fashions, opinions, religions, and calls to war. We chant and march to the group heartbeat, wear its symbols. Also called "Herd Behavior" and "The Bandwagon Effect."

LOOK-ALIKES BIAS

Being attracted to people who resemble us.

We feel cozy, validated and turned on by people who share our physical appearance—nose shape (biggest factor), coloring, height, taste in clothes, and other personal quirks—and feel uneasy around people who look and act different. No wonder lovers and friends look like siblings.

Us and Them

BY ROBERT M. SAPOLSKY

Robert is a professor of biological sciences at Stanford University and of neurology at Stanford's School of Medicine. He is the author of A Primate's Memoir *and* Why Zebras Don't Get Ulcers.

A truly discouraging thing to me is how easily humans see the world as dichotomized between Us and Them. This comes through in all sorts of ways—social anthropology, lord of the flies, prison experiments, linguistics (all those cultures where the word for the members of that culture translates into "People," thus making a contrast with the non-people living in the next valley).

As a neurobiologist, I'm particularly impressed with and discouraged by one finding relevant to this. There's a part of the brain called the *amygdala* that has lots to do with fear and anxiety and aggression. Functional brain imaging studies of humans show that the amygdala becomes metabolically active when we look at a scary face (even when the face is flashed up so quickly that we aren't consciously aware of seeing it). And some recent work—solid, done by top people, independently replicated—suggests that the amygdala can become activated when we view the face of someone from another race. The Them as scary, and the Them being someone whose skin color is real different from our own.

Damn, that's an upsetting finding.

But right on the heels of those studies are follow-ups showing that the picture is more complicated. The "Other skin color = scared activated amygdala = the Other" can be modified by experience. "Experience," can be how diverse of a world you grew up in. More diversity, and the amygdala is likely to become activated in that circumstance. And also, "experience," can be whether, shortly before your amygdala is put through the brain imaging paces, you are subtly biased to think about people categorically or as individuals. If you're cued towards individuating, your amygdala doesn't light up.

Thus, it seems quite plausible to me that we are hardwired towards making Us/Them distinctions and not being all that nice to the Them. But what is anything but hardwired is who counts as an Us and as a Them—we are so easily manipulated into changing those categories.

So, I'm *optimistic* that with the right sort of priorities and human engineering (whatever that phrase means), we can be biased towards making Us/Them dichotomies far more benign than they tend to be now. Say, by making all of us collectively feel like an Us with Them being the space aliens that may attack us some day. Or making the Them to be mean, shitty, intolerant people without compassion.

But, I'm sure not optimistic that we'll soon be having political, religious or cultural leaders likely to move us effectively in that direction. Just to deflate that optimism.

The Letters in Your Name
Are Hidden Persuaders

BY JOHN A. BARGH

John is a Professor of Psychology at Yale University. This essay appears in Are We Free? *edited by John Baer, James Kaufman, and Roy Baumeister, Oxford University Press, 2008.*

It has long been known that we have a strong preference and liking for people who are similar to ourselves in appearance, attitudes, and beliefs, and this plays a significant role in interpersonal attraction. Recent research has shown that this similarity-liking effect extends to new people who resemble significant others such as our parents, although people are not aware of and do not report any such resemblance as a factor in their liking. The similarity effect is so strong, in fact, that it extends even to preferences for places to live and occupational choices that are similar to ourselves in merely superficial ways.

For example, compared to what you'd expect by chance alone, there are more people named Ken who moved to live in Kentucky, Florences who moved to Florida, and more named Louis who moved to St. Louis; there are more Denises and Denises who become dentists and Laura and Lawrences who become lawyers, compared to people with names that do not share letters with these occupations. If your first or last name begins with "H" you are more likely than chance to own a hardware store, and if one of your

98

names begin with "R", you are more likely to own a roofing company, with "C" a computer company and with "T" a travel business.

This is not at all to say that name-letter similarity is the only basis for our choice of domiciles and professions, but that it is a statistically significant influence on those choices. Most people find this, well, surprising, and it is clearly an unconscious influence as no one would claim name-letter overlap as a reason for making these important life choices.

Other superficial similarities, such as sharing a birthday with another person, produce the same powerful effects. Researchers Walton and Cohen manipulated whether their participants had the same birthday or not with a fellow student, described in a (fictitious) newspaper article (which listed the student's birth-date incidentally in a brief biography sideline to the main article) as having just won a prestigious award for mathematical achievement. Compared to the different-birthday condition, those students who shared a birthday with the award-winner actually had higher grades at the end of the semester in their math classes.

What is the basis for such "implicit egotism?"

Evolutionary biologists have traced this tendency back to a "kin selection" bias that gave our genes a further reproductive and survival advantage. This is one of the pillars of "selfish gene" theory in which genes, not we as individuals, are argued to be the unit of natural selection.

According to selfish-gene theory, over evolutionary history we tend to like those who resemble us because they tended to share genes with us—resemblance in appearance was correlated with resemblance in genetic makeup.

And the contemporary social psychological research described above is showing just how powerful this similarity-preference effect is, as it extends to all sorts of features stored within our self-representations, beyond just physical appearance, to our names, our particular birth-dates, and other self-attributes important to our identities.

Dr. Bargh's Wisdom

• The experience of our own behavior in the present seems particularly spontaneous and "free," because we don't experience, at the same time, all of the unconscious influences and impulses that produced that behavior.

• We've learned that feelings of being in control are far more beneficial to our functioning than are feelings of helplessness; thus these subjective feelings of free will are one of the "positive illusions" we hold dear. Yet this benefit is irrelevant to the scientific status or truth-value regarding the actual existence of free will; however positive and adaptive the feeling, it is still an illusion.

• Each of us lives in a difficult to predict present and near future, which includes our own behavior in it, and which therefore makes our behavior feel spontaneous and undetermined—but what we don't experience, yet which are just as real, are the multitude of unconscious influences and determinants of what we think, act, and feel.

• I am interested in the extent to which any and all social psychological phenomena—attitudes and evaluations, emotions, impressions, motivations, social behavior—occur nonconsciously and automatically. One area of research is the application of the nonconscious-motivation idea to the issue of power abuse and corruption. We are finding clear individual differences in automatic reactions to having power, such that some people abuse it for their own selfish gain and others react with greater social responsibility and concern for others.

• The "feeling of free will" is very real, just as real for those scientists who argue against its actual existence as for everyone else, but this strong feeling is an illusion, just as much as we experience the sun moving through the sky, when in fact it is we who are doing the moving.

"I am a brain, my dear Watson,
and the rest of me is a mere appendage."

— SHERLOCK HOLMES

Is Choice an Illusion?

BY DR. GINGER CAMPBELL

Ginger earned her medical degree from the University of Alabama School of Medicine. She has been practicing emergency medicine since 1992. Her long-standing interest in mind-body issues led her to start her popular Brain Science Podcast *in 2006. You can find her podcasts and blogs at http://virginia-campbellmd.com.*

The evidence is overwhelming that the brain makes our decisions and directs our actions. Experiments have also revealed that a surprising amount of decision-making occurs outside of conscious control.

Does that mean that choice is an illusion? The answer to this question has far reaching implications with respect to personal responsibility. But first, let's consider the nature of so-called unconscious decisions.

Except for very simple reflexes (and basic physiological processes, like breathing), almost all unconscious processes begin in consciousness. When you are learning a new skill, you must consciously attend to the details of each step. It is only after you have practiced the activity many times that it becomes automatic (or "unconscious"). This ability to move tasks down into the unconscious is very valuable since we can only attend closely to one task at a time. Thus, learning a complex skill requires mastering one element at a time until these details become automatic.

How does this apply to moral reasoning? Experiments have also shown that many moral choices are in fact unconscious in the sense that people act without really thinking and then justify their choices with retrospective rationalization. So where do the choices come from?

Experiments with small children (and primates) suggest an innate sense of fairness, but much of our moral reasoning appears to be learned, just like we learn to walk and talk. Thus, most healthy people will do the right thing "without thinking," not because choice is an illusion, but because good choices have become automatic.

And the role of culture is critical.

Just as you grow up speaking the language of your parents, you will tend to grow up with their moral values, and/or the values of the culture of your particular time and place. But does growing up in a bad environment excuse a person who makes decisions that harm others? My answer is "no," because most people who grow up in bad environments are still capable of moral reasoning. And the fact that decisions have an unconscious component does not mean that we are not responsible for our choices and actions. *The unconscious parts of our mind reflect what our conscious mind has done or thought in the past.*

Neuroplasticity: Our Changing Brain

Another aspect of contemporary neuroscience that we should consider is *brain plasticity*: the fact that our brains (and minds) can grow and change. This means that with the possible exception of a severe pathology, rehabilitation is not an impossible goal. But it also means that we cannot use our genes, environment, or past history as an excuse for our choices. Current enthusiasm for genetic advances has led to the tendency to exaggerate the role of genetics, however, "genes are not destiny."

We now know that the environment and experience can actually alter which genes are expressed. Fortunately, brain plasticity means that we are not the helpless results of interaction between our genes and our environment. We can choose activities that strengthen our moral behavior just as we can choose to develop other skills.

Some may argue that morality is a "social construct," but so is almost everything else that humans do. In fact, contemporary neuroscience is discovering that our social nature is a very important component of human intelligence. When comparing the behavior of young chimpanzees with human toddlers, the ability to mimic behavior appears to be a crucial difference that allows humans not only to learn more complex behaviors, but also to share them with others. Learning how to get along with others, which is the essence of morality, is one of the most crucial skills that children must learn.

I have argued that a natural element of human learning is for complex skills to become automatic or unconscious, but that does not rob us either of our autonomy or our responsibility. Meanwhile, brain plasticity offers hope that people can learn to behave in socially appropriate ways if adequate rehabilitation methods can be developed.

Before closing, I want to consider the issue of punishment and retribution because many writers seem to assume that if contra-causal free will does not exist, then punishment is inhumane.

Wired for Revenge

I hope I have made it clear that people with normal brain function should be considered responsible for their actions. Thus, punishment is not automatically "wrong," but we should consider whether it works and where it comes from. I will consider these questions in reverse order. Those who envision a system of justice that contains no punishment are not just ignoring human nature, but they are also ignoring what we have learned from studying other primates. People aren't the only ones who get mad when they feel they have been treated unjustly. The use of punishment and retribution seems to be a common adaptive behavior among social primates. Primates seem to be "wired" for revenge. Outsourcing our need for revenge to a community sanctioned body is an important achievement, but its success rests on having a majority of citizens feeling that the system functions fairly.

Thus, I see two problems with going to a pure rehabilitation model of justice. First, criminals (and lawyers) will no doubt find a way to exploit the system. Second, and perhaps more important, most law abiding citizens will be deeply offended by such an arrangement.

While punishment may not always be a complete deterrent, it does factor in to our moral reasoning. From a young age, our exquisite sense of fairness includes a sense of what constitutes fair punishment. This principle applies whether one is the victim or the offender.

Neuroscience can help inform new systems of justice in the future, but there is also the danger that it will be misapplied. It is becoming increasingly important for scientists to become much more involved in their communities, both in explaining their work and making sure that it is not distorted or misrepresented.

Ginger's Key Points

1. The brain directs our choices and actions.

2. Much of what the brain does is automatic (unconscious), but that does not rob of us of autonomy or responsibility.

3. Since complex skills and thoughts become automatic with repetition, it is wise to repeat only those things we want to become habits.

4. Brain plasticity offers hope for rehabilitation, but research in this field has not yet received much attention or funding.

5. The fact that other primates show a sense of fairness and may use punishment to control behavior indicates that these things are not dependent on a belief in free will.

6. Morality does not require free will or any other supernatural beliefs. Just like all other human behaviors, morality is a complex combination of inheritance, environment, and experience.

Quotes on the Brain

"Two neuroscientists working in Australia have found that, when asking people to choose to move either their left or right hands, it was possible to influence their choice by electronically stimulating certain parts of their brains. So, for example, the scientists could force the subjects always to choose to move their left hands. But despite their choice being electronically directed, these patients continued to report that they were freely choosing which hand to move... Thanks to modern neuro-imaging technology, we now know that our minds—our conscious, mental life—are a product of activity in the brain. So even when we have the conscious experience of deciding, our brains have really already taken the decision for us. Free will is an illusion."

—**Stephen Cave**, *Financial Times*, UK

"Our will, quite the opposite of being free, is steady and stable, like an inner gyroscope, and it is the stability and constancy of our non-free will that makes me me and you you, and that also keeps me me and you you."

—**Douglas R. Hofstadter**, *I Am a Strange Loop*

"If free will exists, why do the tallest candidates with the best hair usually win elections? The correlation is incredibly strong. And yet even the most poorly informed voter understands that neither hair nor height have any correlation with competence." —**Scott Adams**, *Dilbert*

"We are mere machines. And machines may not boast, nor feel proud of their performance, nor claim personal merit for it." —**Mark Twain**, *What is Man?*

"Neuroscience brooks no distinction between me and the physical processes of my brain. It rejects the notion of a freely-willed act, because I have no 'will' above and beyond the neurochemical reactions that make me tick."

—**Kathryn Schultz,** *The Nation* (1-9-2006)

"Our decision to take one action as opposed to another relies on the choreography between processes in the prefrontal cortex and a suite of internal states of the body, including changes in heart rate, breathing, temperature, muscle tone and, especially, our feelings. Recurrent encounters with particular objects (and people) and events will create changes in the somato-sensory areas of the brain that function like road maps for bodily action."

—**Marc Hauser,** *Moral Minds*

"You, your joys and your sorrows, your memories and your ambitions, your sense of personal identity and free will, are in fact no more than the behavior of a vast assembly of nerve cells and their associated molecules. As Lewis Carroll's Alice might have said: 'You're nothing but a pack of neurons.'"

—**Francis Crick, Ph.D.**

"To admit that the mind is electrochemical does not diminish our concept of self: rather, it suggests that the cosmos was charged with the possibility of becoming conscious from the first instant of creation."

—**Chet Raymo,** *physicist & astronomer*

"It is tempting to believe that our minds float free of our genomes. But such beliefs are completely at odds with everything that scientists have learned in molecular biology in the past decade."

—**Gary Marcus,** *The Birth of the Mind*

"We don't so much make decisions as our brain makes them for us. When we claim conscious ownership of the actions performed by our brain, we act like the proud parents of a gifted child, taking credit for the child's brilliance even though we only provided the necessary conditions for that brilliance."
—**Richard Restak,** *The Naked Brain*

"We are importantly unpredictable except for our *general tendencies and patterns*. We will go to sleep at night, get up in the morning, tend to hug our spouse at least three or four times a day, but exactly when, or what words will come out of our mouths, that's unpredictable. So we mustn't fear what science seems to tell, that we are just robots."

—**Patricia Churchland, UCSD** *professor of philosophy*

"Good judgment is more than a matter of 'gut feeling' or rational deliberation—it's the willingness to reflect on the [brain's] decision-making process itself."

—**Jonah Lehrer,** *How We Decide*

"Neuroscience is changing the way we think about ourselves. One of the hardest changes for people to assimilate is the idea that our intentional, voluntary behavior is the product of a physical system, the brain. If physical processes in the brain cause our actions, then how can there be free will?"

—**Martha Farah,** Director of the University of Pennsylvania's Center for Cognitive Neuroscience

"The mind is what the brain does."

—**Steven Pinker,** *How the Mind Works*

5.

The Myth & Naturalism

Naturalism re-enchants the physical world.
We don't need the supernatural or non-physical
to account for the marvels of nature,
including ourselves.

BY THOMAS W. CLARK

Tom is the founder and director of the Center for Naturalism, based in Somerville, Massachusetts.

Naturalism is a worldview which holds that there is a single, natural, physical world in which we are completely included. There isn't a separate supernatural or immaterial realm, nor is there anything supernatural or immaterial about us. Naturalism is based on taking science—not faith, revelation, intuition or tradition—as our way of deciding what ultimately exists. One way to understand it is to pose a basic question: How do we explain human behavior? Here are two explanations, one naturalistic, the other not naturalistic:

1. The Free Will Explanation

This explanation involves the traditional view that people, although they may be influenced in many respects, choose their behavior using what philosophers call "contra-causal" free will, a will which is itself not fully determined by anything else. This sort of free will is often thought to be exercised by a non-physical soul or consciousness that's independent of causality. On this view, persons are in some respect first causes, agents who cause things to happen but are not fully caused themselves. To explain behavior we appeal, ultimately, to contra-causal free will, even though we admit there are various factors that influence people's character, motives, impulses and decisions. Having this sort of free will is to be *causally privileged* over nature. It's to be little gods, to be in some important sense self-created, so that we get to take ultimate credit and blame for who we are and what we do.

2. The Scientific Explanation

Science finds no evidence for the existence of the non-physical soul or contra-causal free will, and instead looks at all the factors coming together in someone's behavior, taking the genetics and history of the person into account. It explains why the person is the way she is, and then explains behavior in terms of how she interacts with her current environment. If we replayed the tape of history, with all factors exactly the same, inside and outside the person, the same behavior would have arisen. There's no reason to suppose she could have done otherwise, given the conditions that held at the time.

The first explanation involves something supernatural, namely the freely-willing soul. The second, since it's based in science, is entirely naturalistic. Naturalism denies the existence of gods, ghosts, angels, or non-physical entities that can't be confirmed to exist or be explained by scientific methods. For the same reason, it denies we have souls that have contra-causal free will and that could have done otherwise.

The naturalistic view that we are not little gods, but fully natural, fully caused creatures, is empowering, both personally and socially. Understanding the causal story behind the self and its choices gives us more power to control the circumstances that shape us, inspire creativity, and help realize our goals.

But there's a catch: the person that's getting more power is reconceptualized as a fully caused function of the world surrounding it, not as a first cause. So we don't get to take ultimate credit and blame, to be as egoistical, as prideful, as blaming, or as retributive. Instead, we're led to be more accepting, compassionate and empathetic. People don't create themselves, so responsibility for their character and behavior isn't ultimately theirs, but is distributed over the many factors that shaped them. Were we given their environmental and genetic lot in life, we would have become who they are and acted as they did: *there but for circumstances go I.* What follows are excerpts from Tom Clark's new book, *Encountering Naturalism: A Worldview and Its Uses.*

The Wonderful Inscrutability of Existence

It's easy to see that from a naturalist perspective there cannot be any ultimate purpose to existence: as soon as any purpose is proposed, one can simply ask why that purpose should drive existence, as opposed to some other purpose. Even if a god created us to glorify him and his works, we are still creatures who can ask why god himself exists, and why his purposes should be considered ultimate.

In reacting to the specter of purposelessness, people often insist that there's got to be something more than just space, matter and energy—a driving cosmic intention. But once we've understood the unstable logic of the desire for ultimate meaning, we can begin to savor our position as a very curious one indeed. There's no particular way things are ultimately *meant* to be, so we stand perpetually astonished and wondering.

Seeing that we're temporary players on the stage of existence makes the spectacle all the more compelling. Were we immortal souls, life would lose a great deal of its urgency and value. Think of plastic flowers, which are virtually indestructible but aesthetically empty. Impermanence, not permanence, is what drives our engagement in life.

Liberals vs. Conservatives

Naturalism produces the fundamental insight that our opponents and enemies, whether political, ethnic, religious or otherwise, are not self-created monsters. However misguided we suppose them to be, we can't suppose that, given their genes and circumstances, they could have believed and acted other than they did. Conservatives, for instance, have certain personality traits and predispositions that lead them to support particular policies. Likewise for liberals.

The same lesson applies in the international arena. If, for instance, the Israelis and Palestinians understood each other not as self-created evil-doers who willfully disobey Allah's or Yahweh's commandments, but as products of deterministic social and geo-political processes, this might reduce the mutual hatred that drives conflict in the Middle East. My enemy is who I would have been, but for an accident of birth and culture, so can I continue to regard him as evil incarnate? If not, perhaps we can talk.

The idea that we are little gods, who can choose to act independently of our genes and environmental circumstances, helps to motivate ethnic conflict and genocide. That kind of thinking allows us to deeply blame and resent "the other." We think: They could have risen above their circumstances and been good people like us, if they'd only chosen to, using their free will.

New-Age Magical Thinking

Through its allegiance to empiricism, naturalism counters the pseudo-science and magical thinking of New Age mysticism, not to mention astrology, fortune telling, and other "psychic" arts. Although proponents of the New Age (for instance gurus such as Ken Wilber and Andrew Cohen) like to claim scientific backing for paranormal abilities and "consciousness evolution," there's no solid, peer-reviewed evidence for occult mental powers or for the idea that human consciousness is evolving toward any goal.

Among other things, naturalism is the tough-minded refusal to let our strong desires for meaning and control warp our perception of reality. See Lee Silver's book, *Challenging Nature,* for a bracing rebuttal of all manner of fuzzy thinking about the soul and New Age mysticism.

Hang On to Your Passions

Human persons don't disappear under naturalism, even though we can explain how they originate and develop. Without free will, we remain complex, autonomous creatures, who act for reasons and motives that are legitimately ours, not anyone else's. Your will—expressed in your passions, plans and actions—is just as strong as ever.

If you discover you have a burning desire to save the whales, or all the other species now in danger for extinction, you can join Greenpeace and likely make a difference. All that's changed is that you understand clearly where your desires and powers come from. They aren't ultimately self-caused. In fact, to really understand yourself *requires* understanding the cause-and-effect relationships between events in your life.

Coping with Difficult People

As Spinoza said long ago about determinism: "This doctrine teaches us to hate no one, to despise no one, to mock no one, to be angry with no one, and to envy no one."

The person at the office who drives you crazy with his arrogance is completely a function of his formative and current conditions—including you!—which should give you pause before indulging in revenge fantasies.

Of course, we're all prone to such responses since we evolved to have the capacity for anger and resentment for good reasons: to get those who treat us poorly to shape up. But once we see clearly that those who mistreat us aren't self-made, it's easier to let such feelings go once they stop playing a useful role.

Understanding that people aren't self-made can help heal troubled relationships, since you won't hold grudges for as long, or waste much time resenting someone or plotting to get even. Petty arguments will remain just that, petty, without getting out of control. You'll be able to grin and bear someone's foibles, and maybe even give them useful feedback instead of shunning them or swearing at them.

More to Explore Online

The Center for Naturalism is devoted to increasing public awareness of scientific naturalism and its implications for social and personal well-being. By means of lectures, publications and research, the CFN seeks to foster the understanding that human beings are entirely natural phenomena, and that human flourishing is best achieved in the light of such understanding.

- ◆ Visit CFN's websites at Naturalism.org and CenterforNaturalism.org.
- ◆ Read Thomas W. Clark's book: *Encountering Naturalism: A Worldview & Its Uses.*
- ◆ CFN's Motto: "NATURE IS ENOUGH"

Quotes on Naturalism

"Naturalism is a worldview based on reason and science, without appeal to religious mythologies or mysticism, which can be intelligently applied to improve the human condition. The need for defending naturalism has never been greater, as the dogmatic forces of supernaturalism and superstition continue to exert excessive control over humanity."

—John Shook
Vice President for Research at the Center for Inquiry

"Advances in psychology and neuroscience strongly suggest that the concept of *free will* be abandoned. In fifty years, it may be historically interesting, but practically obsolete. Once you know the science, certain traditional philosophical questions are no longer questions."

—Paul Davies,
*Subjects of the World: Darwin's Rhetoric
and the Study of Agency in Nature*

"Once one's physiology has become integrated enough to see everything 'under the gaze of eternity'—that is, once one has become *enlightened*—one recognizes that free will is only an illusion produced by one's prior inadequate perceptual and conceptual perspective."

—Baruch Spinoza, *philosopher*

"I'm concerned with what's true. For me, the evolution/creation war is really just a battle. It's a skirmish in a larger war between supernaturalism and naturalism."

—Richard Dawkins
The Greatest Show on Earth

"Hey, don't look at me — I was *against* free will."

"Surely there must have been times in high school or college when you laid in bed, late at night, and wondered where your 'free will' came from? What part of the brain is responsible for deciding to act one way or another? One traditional answer is that this is not the job of the brain at all but rather of the soul. Hovering above the brain, the soul freely perturbs the networks for the brain thereby triggering the neural activity that will ultimately lead to behavior.

"Although such dualistic accounts are emotionally reassuring and intuitively satisfying, they break down as soon as one digs a bit deeper. How can this ghost, made out of some kind of metaphysical ectoplasm, influence brain matter without being detected? What sort of laws does Casper follow? Science has abandoned strong dualistic accounts in favor of *natural* explanations."

—Christof Koch
Professor of Cognitive and Behavioral Biology
at California Institute of Technology

"Do you think I know what I am doing, that for one breath or half-breath I belong to myself, as much as a pen knows what it is writing or a ball can guess where it is going?"

—Rumi, *poet*

"Are you breathing yourself? No? Well, maybe you're not thinking yourself or making decisions either. Maybe it (you) doesn't move until it moves, like a breath, like the wind. Are you telling yourself the story of how you are doing it to keep from the awareness that you are nature and are flowing perfectly?"

—Byron Katie
Loving What Is

"The *beauty* of Nature—sunsets, woodlands, fireflies—has elicited religious emotions throughout the ages. We are moved to awe and wonder at the grandeur, the poetry, the richness of natural beauty. It fills us with joy."

—Ursula Goodenough
The Sacred Depths of Nature

6.

The Myth & Me

"If I hadn't spent so much time studying Earthlings,"
said the Tralfamadorian, "I wouldn't have
any idea what was meant by free will.
I've visited 31 inhabited planets in the universe,
and I have studied reports on 100 more.
Only on Earth is there any talk of free will."

—KURT VONNEGUT, Slaughterhouse Five

One hundred years ago, I wouldn't have written this book. Instead, I'd be raising ten kids, milking cows, ironing sheets, sewing on buttons, and baking apricot pies. One hundred years from now, I probably wouldn't have written it either. By then, everyone will know that free will is a myth and illusion. The word will be out, even in the plains of the Serenghetti. Meanwhile, I feel blessed to know the truth ahead of the curve. Here are a few ways my edgy take on free will has transformed me.

I'm more aware of YOU.

Knowing that people don't have free will has made me more appreciative of their joys and sorrows, upbringing and past experiences. I care more about what makes people tick. I am able to empathize on a deeper level.

I puff-up with pride less often.

I still enjoy taking credit for my accomplishments, yet have noticed that my feelings of pride often shift into feelings of gratitude. I feel blessed to have a brain that enables me to accomplish my goals and grateful for the hundreds of people and products that assist me along the way: my husband, parents, friends, teachers, culture, and computer.

I blame others less.

The myth of free will thrives on blame. Since I've abandoned it, I'm much more accepting of people's behaviors. Instead of casting blame and acting self-righteous, I try to understand a person's frame of reference, where they are coming from. Sometimes, I ask questions that take people deeper into their values. I might inquire about the origin of a particular viewpoint. I'm more inquisitive, less derisive.

I frequently reflect on my choices.

I understand that what I choose at any given moment is heavily constrained by what I have chosen before. My current choices are simply altered versions of earlier ones, so I don't ever choose totally from scratch. Furthermore, I understand that many of my choices have immediate rewards and are not necessarily options that might benefit me in the future. This humbles me. I like what Albert Camus said about self-reflection: "An intellectual is someone whose mind watches itself." I certainly think more about my thinking and what motivates me. Meditating has become more enjoyable and easier, too.

I think about my habits differently.

I routinely read at certain cafés, order certain foods and drinks, and meet with certain friends. Without habits, I would have to figure out *everything* from scratch—and my brain would go on strike from overwork. I'm intrigued by what brain researcher Gerard Roth of the University of Bremen says about habits: "The brain is always trying to automate things and to create habits, which imbues it with feelings of pleasure. Holding onto the tried-and-true gives us a feelings of security, safety, and competence while at the same time reducing our fear of the future and of failure." So our habits make us feel more secure in an insecure world.

People annoy me far less.

In the grips of the myth of free will, I was far less tolerant of people's irritating behaviors. Now when someone bugs me, I remind myself that he or she (like me) has no more free agency than a hurricane.

I've become a neuroscience junkie.

I've accepted that most of my options are weighed in my unconscious mind, and that I'm largely in the dark about why (and how) one is chosen over another. To learn more about unconscious decision-making, I read books like these bestselling gems: *Kluge, Nudge, Sway, Hidden Brain, Predictably Irrational, How We Decide, A Mind of It's Own, Quirkology, The Drunkard's Walk, Heuristics & Biases, Don't Believe Everything You Think, Neuro Revolution, Hardwired Behavior,* and *Best of the Brain from Scientific American.*

I'm less apologetic.

I worry less about my screw-ups. I'm less self-accusatory and guilt-ridden. I understand that everything I do has a lengthy, circuitous and mysterious history, so ultimately nothing I do can be called a mistake. *I did what I did.* Sure, I might respond more intelligently in a similar situation in the future. But perhaps I won't. I can't know.

I love evolutionary perspectives.

I'm reading *Evolution for Everyone* by David Sloan Wilson and *The Most Dangerous Animal: Human Nature and the Origins of War* by David Livingston Smith. I want to know more about the ways my hunter-gatherer ancestors coped and what lead to the emergence of our "sense of self" and the illusion of free will. When did free will become a collective story? What advantages did it give people in a (relatively) less civilized world?

I'm less defensive.

Because I take people's criticisms less personally, I engage in fewer counter-attacks. I'm more detached and open. Instead of being reactive, I think: What is he needing me to say or do right now? And what could work for both of us?

I'm not a depressed nihilist.

Some people tell me, "If you drop your belief in free will, you'll become a *nihilist* and fall into a deep state of despair." It didn't happen. I create meaning in my life and feel highly significant. I love being a part of the human drama.

I'm less vulnerable to brainwashing.

Understanding determinism had made me more aware of people's attempts to influence my thoughts and feelings, to sell me stuff I don't need. I'm more conscious of advertisers, teachers (gurus, healers, workshop leaders, and self-help books), religious converters, government propaganda, and the unbridled enthusiasms of well-meaning friends.

Also, I've noticed two types of brainwashing: *internal* and *external*. I see my genetic likes-and-dislikes as internal brainwashing. By contrast, my culture's memes are external brainwashing. Overall, I'm less easily duped. I find myself saying "no" without feeling guilty.

I cheat less.

I'm a pleaser—too much of one!—which has always made cheating difficult. Nonetheless, submerging my mind in deterministic messages, for the past four years, has made me even more honest. I'm less tempted to cheat because I experience each human as a family member (more of the time), belonging to a species blessed and cursed with an advanced brain, each with a similar assemblage of neurons and their associated molecules buffeting them around.

I adore the concept of "causality."

Sometimes, I seek a few obvious causes for my actions, even though most are hidden and can't be known. I like what Buddha said: "All things appear and disappear because of the concurrence of causes and conditions. Nothing ever exists entirely alone. Everything is in relation to everything else."

I've stopped trying to change people.

I knew the myth had lost its grip when I stopped trying to change people. Instead of attempting personality makeovers, I remind myself: "If changing is so easy, you do it—lose ten pounds, eat fewer bags of Barbara's Cheese Puffs." I will ask people to make small adjustments. But I set more reasonable boundaries and am less attached to the outcome. And when someone disappoints me, I get over it sooner.

I'm a better listener (a major feat).

Before my free-will research, I was a self-centered listener, like most people I know. (Good listeners are an endangered species.) I focused more on my own mind-blather and felt entitled to switch the topic to something that riveted me, not realizing that most people find their own stories, no matter how dull or inane, more fascinating than mine.

I'm fascinated by the role of luck.

"People are afraid to face how great a part of life is dependent on luck. It's scary to think so much is out of one's control," said Woody Allen in *Matchpoint*. Luck gave me a $1,000 UCLA Alumni Scholarship because the girl in first place got pregnant and was disqualified. I was in second place. Luck gave me U.S. citizenship. I could have been born in Somalia instead of California. Luck gave me life. Betty, my mom, had an abortion two months before I was conceived. Luck introduced me to my husband Dave. If I hadn't worked as a dental hygienist at Dr. Hazlett's office, I never would have met him. Here's to lucky breaks!

126

I'm here to play my part.

I'm happy with the part the universe has given me to play and don't mind that my choices are constrained by my genes and conditioning and brain state. I'll never become an opera singer or bulldozer operator. Sure, I can rebel and stop doing what I'm designed to do, but that would feel bizarre, cause discomfort. More than ever, I'm content being me, a lithe blonde in her sixties who wants to live to be one-hundred, so she can write more books and travel to more exotic places on this scenic, highly-entertaining planet.

My wish for YOU.

My hope is that you will love, cherish and embrace your life without a belief in free will. If you drop it, you may find yourself thinking: "Since I don't have free will, I'll read up on neuroscience and meditation, learn more about my unique brain. I'll think about how I'm wired, get to know myself on a cellular level." Metacognition is power.

I also hope you will think more about excessive *pride* and *blame* and *greed*. These self-focused behaviors, I believe, are enhanced by the myth of free will.

Finally, I feel blessed that my path led me to the essays and quotes in this book and to the brilliant, witty authors who wrote them. And, most of all, I feel grateful that you chose to join me on this journey. I hope you will share this book with your friends, so together we may create a more compassionate world.

The Quiz Revisited

Now that you've finished reading, you can look at the notes you made and see if your thinking has been influenced by what you've read.

- Has your definition of free will changed?
- Do you still think you have free will? If so, why?
- Do you understand causality and determinism?
- Do you still think the myth has benefits?
- Do you understand the costs of the belief?

TRY THIS: At the end of a day, make a list of 20 things you did. Review it and ask: "What did I do that wasn't typically me?" Did you do anything that was totally out of character? Place a checkmark by these activities. That leaves the activities that are more you. I like this exercise because it enables me to see how much my genes and past experiences guide me throughout the day. Also, it keeps me in touch with my ruts, habits and comfort zones.

Glossary

caused, causal, causality We behave the way we do because of the various causes that shape us, whether these are genetic or environmental. We don't have the capacity to act outside of the causal connections that link us in every respect to the rest of the world.

• *contra-causal* Contra-causal means "against causality or the law of cause-and-effect." Free will, as many people think of it, is a contra-causal power.

conditioning Our life experiences and environmental input—what we learn from our parents, peers, schooling, culture, generation, social status, and historical time-slot.

decision-making The cognitive process leading to the selection of a course of action among alternatives. The anterior cingulate cortex and orbitofrontal cortex are brain regions involved in decision-making.

determinism The view that every event, without exception, is causally determined by prior events. Human thoughts and actions are events. Therefore, human thoughts and actions are, without exception, causally determined by prior events.

dualism The term 'dualism' has a variety of uses in the history of thought. In general, the idea is that, for some particular domain, there are two kinds of things. In the philosophy of mind, dualism is the theory that the mental and physical—or the mind and body or mind and brain—are two different kinds of things. The brain is natural and the mind is supernatural.

• *Cartesian Dualism:* René Descartes (1641) held that the mind is a nonphysical substance. He was the first to clearly identify the mind with consciousness and self-awareness and to distinguish this from the brain, which was the seat of intelligence.

existentialists People who accept that, while no meaning has been designed into the universe, we can each creatively provide meaning for ourselves. Author Susan Blackmore says, "We humans can, and do, make up our own purposes, but *ultimately* the universe has none. All the wonderfully complex and beautifully designed things we see around us were built by the same purposeless process—evolution by natural selection."

fatalism The belief that all events are predetermined and therefore inevitable, that something will happen no matter what we do. A submissive attitude. By contrast, *determinism* leaves "us" in the picture, so that what we do matters.

free will The view that humans have a "spirit" or "soul" or "some magical quality" that can control the brain's decision-making circuitry. This airy, ghostly, shadowy, supernatural agent can—when it feels like it!—override our genes and conditioning, so we may act randomly. The doctrine of free will denies the law of cause-and-effect and states that humans are first causes or little gods with the power to make genuinely unconstrained choices.

ghost in the machine A derogatory phrase that refers to the presence of a "self," "spirit," or "soul" that directs the brain. British philosopher Gilbert Ryle's description for Rene Descartes' mind-body dualism: Mental activity is of a different category from physical activity.

habits Automatic routines of behavior that are repeated regularly, often without thinking. When we choose familiar things, an area deep in our brain, the basal ganglia, fires an exact sequence. When we do something new, a very different brain area, the prefrontal cortex, fires up.

indeterminism The stance that not all events have identifiable causes. The theory that the will is to some extent independent of motives.

libertarian free will The school of thought claiming that free will and determinism are incompatible. Humans are free agents. To put it tastefully, it means the whole chain of cause-and-effect in the history of the universe stops dead in its tracks as you pick an ice cream flavor.

metacognition Thinking about thinking. The brain is able to reflect on its own contents, thoughts and feelings. This complex human skill feeds the illusion of free will.

naturalism A worldview that says nature is all there is and nothing supernatural exists. It inspires a deep love for the natural world, which includes us. Go to *The Center for Naturalism* for an introduction: CenterforNaturalism.org.

neuroscience Any of the sciences, such as neurochemistry and experimental psychology, that deal with the structure or function of the nervous system and brain.
• *Mirror Neurons:* Nerve cells in the brain specialized for empathy, learning and imitation.

supernaturalism A doctrine that teaches people to believe in entities and processes that defy the laws of nature: gods, angels, ghosts, souls, aliens, psychics, yada, yada.

Acknowledgments

First and foremost, I would like to thank all of the authors of the essays featured in this anthology: Susan Blackmore, Richard Dawkins, Sam Harris, Daniel Dennett, Michael Shermer, Daniel Wegner, Steven Pinker, William B. Provine, Ginger Campbell, Laurence Tancredi, John A. Bargh, V. S. Ramachandran, Clay Shirky, Tamler Sommers, Robert Sapolsky, and Lee M. Silver. Without your research and wisdom, this book would not exist. Thank you for granting me permission to share your wonderful words.

I owe a special debt of gratitude to Tom Clark who has a deep understanding of free will, causality and morality. His kindness and support inspired me to create this third revised edition of the book. I would also like to thank Arnell Dowret for his contribution to the book.

Thanks also goes to my husband, Dave, who tolerated this long and demanding project with grace, even though he had little interest in chatter about "living without free will." He made this project possible by providing me with a serene and beautiful workspace on a verdant island in the Pacific, and by feeding me lots of homegrown fruits and veggies.

Finally, I would like to thank and praise Ramesh Balsekar and Byron Katie for living happily and morally in a continuous state of nondoership, and for tirelessly sharing their experience, via talks and books, with thousands of people throughout the world.

References

Adams, Scott. *God's Debris: A Thought Experiment.* (New York: Andrews McMeel), 2001. Dilbert.blog.

Balsekar, Ramesh. *Peace and Harmony in Daily Living.* Mumbai: Yogi Impressions, 2003.

Bargh, John. "Free will Is Un-natural." *Are We Free?* edited by Baer, Kaufman and Baumeister. (Oxford University Press, 2008)

P 22 Berthoz, Alain. *Emotion & Reason.* (Oxford University Press, 2003), 65.

Blackmore, Susan. *What We Believe but Cannot Prove.* (New York: Harper, 2006), pp. 40-41. *Conversations on Consciousness.* (Oxford University Press, 2006), 63. *Ten Zen Questions.* (Oxford: One World Publications, 2009).

Bloom, Paul. *Descartes Baby.* (NY: Basic Books, 2004). Quote from *Seed* magazine, June-July '06, 20.

Campbell, Ginger. *Her essay was written for this book.*

Camus, Albert (1913-1960). June 1941, *Notebooks 1935-1942*, tr. Philip Thody, 1963.

Cave, Stephen. "I Think Therefore I Am, I Think." FT.com Financial Times. 4/12/07

Clark, Thomas W. *Encountering Naturalism.* (Somerville, MA: Center for Naturalism, 2007), 19, 20, 33, 46-49, 55, 56. Go to CenterforNaturalism.org

Cronin, Helena. "Getting Human Nature Right," a chapter in *The New Humanists,* edited by John Brockman. (New York: Barnes and Noble Books, 2003), 57

Darwin, Charles. *Charles Darwin's Notebooks,* 1836-1844. (Cornell University Press), 608.

Davies, Paul. "Undermining Free Will." *Foreign Policy,* 36. September-October 2004.

Dawkins, Richard. Essay from Edge.org.

Dennett, Daniel C. *Freedom Evolves.* (New York: Penguin Putnam, 2003), 1, 10, 13.

Dowret, Arnell. Onewitheverything.org. Tenet 3. "Human behavior is the result of causes."

Einstein, Albert. "Our actions..." Statement to the Spinoza Society, 9/22/32. Einstein Archive, 33-291.

Emerson, Ralph W. "Circles;" "Compensation." Essays, First Series, 1841.

Flanagan, Owen. *The Problem of the Soul.* (New York: Perseus Books, 2002), 128.

Gazzaniga, Michael S. *The Ethical Brain.* (New York: Dana Press, 2005), 102, 146-147.

Greene, Joshua. *Discover* magazine. "Whose Life Would You Save?" April 2004.

Goodenough, Ursula. *The Sacred Depths of Nature.* (Oxford University Press, 1998), xvi

Harris, Sam. 2005. *The End of Faith.* (New York: W. W. Norton), 272-274.

Hauser, Marc D. *Moral Minds: How Nature Designed Our Universal Sense of Right and Wrong.* (New York: HarperCollins, 2006), xvii, 31, 228.

Hofstadter, Douglas. *I Am In A Strange Loop.* (New York: Basic Books, 2007), 341.

Ingersoll, Robert Green. *Ingersoll the Magnificent* by Joseph Lewis. (Austin: American Atheist Press, 1985).

Isaacson, Walter. *Einstein.* (New York: Simon & Schuster, 2007). "Einstein & Faith." *Time.* April 5, 2007.

Kandel, Eric, Quote from an interview with Charlie Rose.

Katie, Byron. *A Thousand Names for Joy.* (New York: Harmony Books, 2007), 47

Koch, Christof. "The Will to Power." *Scientific American Mind* magazine, November/December 2009, p. 20.

Lehrer, Jonah. *How We Decide.* (New York: Houghton Mifflin Harcourt, 2009), 76-78; Also, *Seed Magazine*, "Thinking Meta." February 2009, 58. 59.

Ludden, David. "Born to Believe." *Skeptical Inquirer* magazine. January/February 2008, p. 53.

Marcus, Gary. *The Birth of the Mind.* (New York: Basic Books, 2004), p. 86.

Metzinger, Thomas. "The Forbidden Fruit Intuition."
What Is Your Dangerous Idea? edited by John Brockman.
(NY: Harper Perennial, 2007), 143-4.

Montague, Read. *Why Choose this Book?* (New York:
Dutton, 2006) viii

Osho. *Zen: It's History and Teachings.* (UK: The
BridgewaterBook Co., 2004), 137.

Pigliucci, Massimo. "Can There Be a Science of Free
Will?" *Skeptical Inquirer*, Volume 31, Issue 3, 26.

Pinker, Steven. *The Blank Slate. (*New York: Penguin
Books, 2002), 53, 131, 174-5, 184-5."How to Think
about the Mind." *Newsweek*, September 27, 2004, p. 78.

Provine, William B. "The Myth of Free Will and Its Evil
Consequences." Lecture to the Santa Fe Institute on
March 20, 2003.

Ramachandran, V. S. From John Brockman's book, *What Is
Your Dangerous Idea?* (New York: Harper Perennial, 2007).
Phantom in the Brain. (New York: Harper Perennial, 1991),
22-26.

Raymo, Chet. *Skeptics and True Believers: The Exhilarating
Connection between Science and Religion.* (New York: Walker
& Company, 1998), 194-195.

Roth, Gerard. *Scientific American Mind*, January 2009, 48

Sapolsky, Robert M. From John Brockman's anthology,
What Are You Optimistic About? (New York: Harper

Perennial, 2007), pp. 91-92.

Schlinger, Henry D. "How the Human Got Its Mind."
Skeptic magazine, Volume 11, Number 4, 2005; 48.

Shermer, Michael. From John Brockman's book, *What We
Believe but Cannot Prove.* (New York: Harper
Perennial, 2006), pp. 38-39.

Shirky, Clay. From John Brockman's book, *What Is Your
Dangerous Idea?* (New York: Harper, 2007).

Shook, John. "Naturalism Research Project Launched at
Center for Inquiry," *Skeptical Inquirer*, p. 27, Feb./Mar.
2007.

Silver, Lee M. *Challenging Nature: The Clash of Science and
Spirituality at the New Frontiers of Life.* (New York:
HarperCollins, 2006), 58-61, 64.

Sommers, Tamler. *The Believer* magazine; March 2003.
www.believermag.com

Spinoza, Baruch. *Ethics* (proposition III, part II). In R. H.
M. Elwes, Spinoza: *The chief works* (vol. 2, p. 134). New
York: Dover.

Strawson, Galen. *The Believer* magazine interview. "You
Cannot Make Yourself the Way You Are." August
2006.

Tancredi, Laurence. *Hardwired Behavior.* (Cambridge
University Press, 2005), 34, 41-42, 74-75, 116.

Warnekan, Feliz. *Science News*, "Ape Aid." June 30, 2007,
Vol. 171, p. 406.

Wegner, Daniel M. *The Illusion of Conscious Will*
(Cambridge: MIT Press, 2002), adapted from
1-2, 27, 28, 341-342.

Wolpert, Lewis. *Six Impossible Things Before Breakfast*,
(New York; W.W. Norton, 2006), 51

Zimbardo, Philip. *The Lucifer Effect*. (New York: Random
House, 2007`) p. 5

CRIS EVATT is a passionate simplifier of both her material and mental life. She tosses out the extraneous wherever it lurks and keeps coming back to bare essentials. In this book, she aims her sights on simplifying "free will" for a mainstream audience, the biggest challenge of her writing career. Previously she targeted closets, kitchens, home offices and interpersonal relationships. She calls herself a "freethinker" with a naturalistic worldview. She is committed to science, which she believes provides the best way to understand the world. On the job front, she has been a blackjack dealer at Lake Tahoe, a dental hygienist in San Francisco, and a co-owner of a Marin County entertainment magazine. In the eighties, she and her husband Dave sailed their 43-foot sloop "Pursuit" from Sausalito to The Fiji Islands. She attended UCLA for three years and graduated from Northwestern University. She is the coauthor of *The Givers & the Takers* and *30 Days to a Simpler Life*.